Fruits!

A Fruit Cookbook with Delicious Recipes
for Cooking with Fruits

By
BookSumo Press

Published by
http://www.booksumo.com

LEGAL NOTES

Table of Contents

Strawberry Shortcake 101

🥄 Prep Time: 20 mins
🕐 Total Time: 20 mins

Servings per Recipe: 12	
Calories	296.8
Fat	11.5g
Cholesterol	20.8mg
Sodium	235.3mg
Carbohydrates	46.5g
Protein	3.7g

Ingredients

1 quart fresh strawberries
1/2 C. sugar
8 oz. cream cheese, softened
1 C. powdered sugar
1 (8 oz.) containers frozen whipped topping
1 (14 oz.) angel food cake, cut into cubes

Directions

1. Wash, stem and halve the strawberries.
2. In a bowl, add the strawberries and sugar and toss to coat well.
3. Refrigerate to chill.
4. In another bowl, add the cream cheese and powdered sugar and beat well.
5. Fold in the whipped topping and cake cubes.
6. Place the cake into an ungreased 13x9-inch baking dish.
7. Refrigerate, covered for at least 2 hours.
8. Cut the chilled cake into squares and serve with the topping of the strawberries.

I ♥ STRAWBERRY
Drinks

Prep Time: 5 mins
Total Time: 5 mins

Servings per Recipe: 2
Calories	161.8
Fat	2.4g
Cholesterol	8.5mg
Sodium	32.7mg
Carbohydrates	33.4g
Protein	2.4g

Ingredients

1 C. strawberry, sliced
1/2 C. milk
1/2 C. water
1/4 C. caster sugar
1/2-2/3 tsp vanilla

Directions

1. Slice up enough fresh strawberries to fill one cup.
2. In a food processor, add strawberries and remaining Ingredients and pulse till smooth.

Bread
for Brunch

Prep Time: 15 mins
Total Time: 1 hr 15 mins

Servings per Recipe: 10

Calories	283.7
Fat	12.7g
Cholesterol	67.5mg
Sodium	272.6mg
Carbohydrates	39.0g
Protein	3.9g

Ingredients

1 3/4 C. flour
1/2 tsp baking powder
1/4 tsp baking soda
1/2 tsp salt
1/4 tsp cinnamon
1/2 C. butter, softened
3/4 C. sugar

1/4 C. light brown sugar
2 eggs, room temperature
1/2 C. sour cream, room temperature
1 tsp vanilla
1 1/4 C. strawberries, fresh & coarsely chopped
3/4 C. walnuts (optional)

Directions

1. Set your oven to 350 degrees F before doing anything else and grease an 8x4-inch loaf pan.
2. In a large bowl, mix together the flour, baking powder, baking soda, salt and cinnamon and keep aside.
3. In small bowl, add the butter and beat till creamy.
4. Slowly, add the sugar, beating continuously till light and airy.
5. Add the brown sugar and mix well.
6. Add the eggs, one at a time, beating continuously till well combined.
7. Add the sour cream and vanilla and beat till well combined.
8. Add the flour mixture and mix till just moistened.
9. Fold in the strawberries and walnuts.
10. Transfer the mixture into the prepared loaf pan.
11. Cook in the oven for about 60-65 minutes.
12. Remove from the oven and keep onto wire rack for about 10 minutes.
13. Carefully, invert the cakes onto wire rack to cool completely.

WEEKEND
Breakfast Muffins

Prep Time: 10 mins
Total Time: 35 mins

Servings per Recipe: 1
Calories	242.6
Fat	9.0g
Cholesterol	52.7mg
Sodium	297.1mg
Carbohydrates	37.1g
Protein	3.7g

Ingredients

2 C. flour
2 tbsp baking powder
1/2 tsp salt
1 C. sugar
6 tsp sugar
1 1/2 C. chopped strawberries

2 eggs
1/2-1 C. unsalted butter, melted
1/2 C. milk
1 tsp vanilla extract

Directions

1. Set your oven to 375 degrees F before doing anything else and line the cups of muffin pans with the paper liners.
2. In a large bowl, mix together the flour, baking powder, salt and 1 C. of the sugar.
3. Add the strawberries and toss to coat well.
4. In another bowl, add the eggs, butter, milk and vanilla and beat till well combined.
5. Add the egg mixture Ingredients to the flour mixture and mix till just combined.
6. Transfer the mixture into the prepared muffin cups evenly and sprinkle with 1/2 tsp of the sugar evenly.
7. Cook in the oven for about 25 minutes or till a toothpick inserted in the center comes out clean.

John the Juice
Smoothie

Prep Time: 5 mins
Total Time: 5 mins

Servings per Recipe: 1

Calories	168.4
Fat	6.1g
Cholesterol	22.7mg
Sodium	83.6mg
Carbohydrates	23.8g
Protein	5.7g

Ingredients

1 1/2 C. milk
1 C. strawberry
2 tbsp sugar
1 tsp lemon juice
1 C. crushed ice

Directions

1. In a blender, add all the Ingredients and pulse till smooth.

GRACE'S
Strawberry Jam

Prep Time: 30 mins
Total Time: 45 mins

Servings per Recipe: 1
Calories	997.7
Fat	0.9g
Cholesterol	0.8mg
Sodium	23.8mg
Carbohydrates	256.3g
Protein	1.3g

Ingredients

2 quarts strawberries, cut and crushed
to yield 5 C. crushed berries
7 C. sugar
1/2 tsp butter
1 (1 3/4 oz.) boxes pectin

Directions

1. In a bowl, place the sugar and keep aside.
2. In a large boiler, place the crushed berries.
3. Add the package of Sure-Jell and mix.
4. Add the butter and bring to a boil.
5. Add the sugar and cook, stirring continuously.
6. Again bring to a boil and boil for about 1 minute, stirring continuously.
7. Remove from the heat and with a metal spoon, skim foam from the top.
8. Immediately, transfer the mixture into the cleaned and preheated jars.
9. With clean hot cloth, clean the rims of the jars.
10. Place the heated lids on jars and tighten the rings.
11. Arrange the jars in water bath canner for about 5 minutes.
12. Remove the jars from canner and turn them upside down for about 5 minutes.
13. Return the jars to upright position and keep in room temperature to cool completely before storing.

Northern California Lemonade

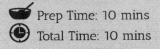 Prep Time: 10 mins

Total Time: 10 mins

Servings per Recipe: 8
Calories	100.6
Fat	0.2g
Cholesterol	0.0mg
Sodium	16.2mg
Carbohydrates	25.8g
Protein	0.5g

Ingredients

3 C. water, cold
1 quart fresh strawberries
3/4 C. sugar
3/4 C. lemon juice
2 C. club soda, cold
Lemon slice (optional)

Directions

1. In a blender, add the water, strawberries and sugar and pulse till smooth.
2. Add the lemon juice and soda and pulse till combined.
3. Serve immediately with a garnishing of the lemon slices.

5-INGREDIENT
Strawberry Crisp

Prep Time: 10 mins
Total Time: 25 mins

Servings per Recipe: 2
Calories	256.8
Fat	7.3g
Cholesterol	15.2mg
Sodium	60.3mg
Carbohydrates	46.7g
Protein	3.2g

Ingredients

1 tbsp butter
1/2 C. uncooked oatmeal
1/4 C. packed brown sugar
1/2 tsp cinnamon
1 C. sliced strawberry

Directions

1. Set your oven to 375 degrees F before doing anything else.
2. In a small pan, melt the butter on low heat.
3. Add the oatmeal, brown sugar and cinnamon and mix well.
4. Immediately, remove from the heat.
5. Place the strawberries in 2 oven-proof dishes evenly and top with the oatmeal mixture.
6. Cook in the oven for about 15 minutes.

Perfect
Strawberry Topping

Prep Time: 10 mins
Total Time: 20 mins

Servings per Recipe: 12
Calories	58.6
Fat	0.2g
Cholesterol	0.0mg
Sodium	13.8mg
Carbohydrates	14.7g
Protein	0.5g

Ingredients

2 lb. ripe strawberries, hulled
1/2 C. granulated sugar
2 tsp cornstarch
1/2 lemon, juice of
1 pinch salt

Directions

1. In a medium pan, mix together all the Ingredients on medium-low heat and cook for about 10 minutes, stirring gently.
2. Remove from heat and keep aside to cool.

ZANZIBAR
Pie

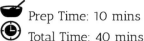

Prep Time: 10 mins
Total Time: 40 mins

Servings per Recipe: 6
Calories   343.4
Fat   10.3g
Cholesterol   98.0mg
Sodium   308.6mg
Carbohydrates   58.7g
Protein   5.4g

Ingredients

3 eggs, beaten
2 1/2 C. rhubarb, red, 1 inch slices
1 1/4 C. sugar
1 1/2 C. strawberries, fresh, sliced
1/4 C. enriched flour
1 9" pastry crust with lattice top

1/4 tsp salt
1 tbsp butter
1/2 tsp nutmeg
Whole strawberries, as required

Directions

1. Set your oven to 400 degrees F before doing anything else.
2. In a large bowl, add the eggs, sugar, flour, salt and nutmeg and mix well.
3. In another bowl, mix together the rhubarb and sliced strawberries.
4. Arrange the pastry crust into a 9-inch pie dish.
5. Place the strawberry mixture over the crust evenly and top with the egg mixture evenly.
6. Place the butter on top in the form of dots.
7. Arrange the lattice crust on top, crimping the edge high.
8. Cook in the oven for about 40 minutes.
9. Fill the openings of the lattice crust with whole strawberries.
10. Serve warm.

Artisanal
Syrup

Prep Time: 10 mins
Total Time: 15 mins

Servings per Recipe: 1
Calories	738.9
Fat	0.4g
Cholesterol	0.0mg
Sodium	3.3mg
Carbohydrates	189.9g
Protein	1.0g

Ingredients

1 pint fresh strawberries
2 C. sugar
1/4 tsp lemon juice

Directions

1. In a food processor, add the strawberries and pulse till smooth.
2. Through a wire-mesh strainer, strain the strawberry puree into a pan
3. Discard the seeds.
4. In the pan, add the sugar and juice on low heat and cook till the sugar dissolves, stirring continuously.
5. Increase the heat to medium-high and bring to a boil.
6. Reduce the heat and simmer for about 5 minutes, skimming the froth from the top.
7. Remove from the heat and keep aside to cool.

LUNCH BOX
Salad

Prep Time: 35 mins
Total Time: 45 mins

Servings per Recipe: 18
Calories   345.4
Fat   15.9g
Cholesterol   34.2mg
Sodium   499.3mg
Carbohydrates   48.2g
Protein   4.4g

Ingredients

2 C. crushed pretzels
3/4 C. butter, melted
3 tbsp white sugar
1 (8 oz.) packages cream cheese,
softened
1 C. white sugar

1 (8 oz.) cartons frozen whipped topping,
thawed
2 (3 oz.) packages strawberry gelatin
2 C. boiling water
2 (10 oz.) packages frozen strawberries

Directions

1. Set your oven to 400 degrees F before doing anything else.
2. In a bowl, add the crushed pretzels, melted butter and 3 tbsp of the white sugar and mix till well combined.
3. In the bottom of 13x9-inch baking dish, place the pretzel mixture and press to smooth the surface.
4. Cook in the oven for about 8-10 minutes.
5. Remove from the oven and keep aside to cool.
6. In a large bowl, add the cream cheese and white sugar and beat till creamy.
7. Fold in the whipped topping.
8. Place the cream cheese mixture over the cooled crust.
9. In a bowl of the boiling water, dissolve the gelatin.
10. Stir in the frozen strawberries and keep aside to set slightly.
11. Place the strawberry mixture over the cream cheese mixture evenly.
12. Refrigerate till set completely.

Mediterranean Strawberries

🥣 Prep Time: 15 mins
🕐 Total Time: 2 hr 15 mins

Servings per Recipe: 6
Calories	39.9
Fat	0.1g
Cholesterol	0.0mg
Sodium	1.8mg
Carbohydrates	9.6g
Protein	0.4g

Ingredients

1 pint ripe strawberry
2 tbsp sugar
2 tbsp balsamic vinegar

Directions

1. Hull the strawberries and cut into quarters lengthwise.
2. In a bowl, add the strawberries, vinegar and sugar and toss to coat well.
3. Cover the bowl and keep aside for about 1 hour.
4. Now, refrigerate to chill for about 1 hour.
5. Remove from the refrigerator and toss again before serving.

FRUITY
Nachos

Prep Time: 1 hr 30 mins
Total Time: 1 hr 38 mins

Servings per Recipe: 6
Calories	284.3
Fat	14.0g
Cholesterol	22.8mg
Sodium	234.4mg
Carbohydrates	37.0g
Protein	4.5g

Ingredients

3 C. sliced fresh strawberries
1/4 C. sugar
1/4 C. apple juice
3/4 C. sour cream
2 tbsp sugar
1/4 tsp cinnamon
6 6-inch flour tortillas

2 tbsp melted butter
2 tsp sugar
1/4 tsp cinnamon
2 tbsp sliced almonds, toasted
1 tbsp shaved semisweet chocolate

Directions

1. In a bowl, add the strawberries, 1/4 C. of the sugar and apple juice and mix well.
2. Refrigerate, covered for at least 1 hour.
3. In another bowl, add the sour cream, 2 tbsp of the sugar and 1/4 tsp of the cinnamon and mix till well combined.
4. Refrigerate, covered till using.
5. Set your oven to 400 degrees F.
6. With a pastry brush, lightly coat 1 side of the tortillas with the melted butter.
7. Cut each tortilla into 6 equal sized wedges.
8. Place the tortilla wedges onto 2 ungreased baking sheets in a single layer and sprinkle with 2 tsp of the sugar and 1/4 tsp of the cinnamon.
9. Cook in the oven for about 6-8 minutes.
10. Remove from the oven and keep aside to cool.
11. Remove the strawberries from the refrigerator and drain completely.
12. Divide the tortilla wedges into 6 dessert bowls and top with the strawberries and a little of the sour cream mixture.
13. Serve with a topping of the toasted almonds and shaved chocolate.

Fiesta
Strawberries

🥣 Prep Time: 45 mins
🕐 Total Time: 45 mins

Servings per Recipe: 15
Calories   343.6
Fat   13.1g
Cholesterol   16.6mg
Sodium   281.8mg
Carbohydrates   53.6g
Protein   4.6g

Ingredients

1 angel food cake
1 (16 oz.) containers Cool Whip
8 oz. cream cheese
1 C. sugar, divided
1 tsp vanilla extract
1 quart fresh strawberries, sliced
3 tbsp cornstarch

1 (3 oz.) packages strawberry Jell-O gelatin dessert
1 tbsp lemon juice
1 C. water

Directions

1. In a medium pan, add 1/2 C. of the sugar, cornstarch, Jell-O, lemon juice and water on medium heat and cook till mixture becomes thick, stirring continuously.
2. Remove from the heat and keep aside to cool slightly.
3. Add the sliced strawberries and stir to combine.
4. Torn the angel food cake into 1-inch pieces.
5. In a bowl, add the cake pieces and 2 C. of the Cool Whip and toss to coat.
6. In another bowl, add the cream cheese, 1/2 C. of the remaining sugar and vanilla and beat till smooth.
7. Stir in the remaining Cool Whip.
8. In a 13x9-inch baking dish, place the cake mixture and press to smooth the surface.
9. Place the cream cheese mixture over the cake mixture evenly and top with the cooled strawberry mixture.
10. Refrigerate for about 2-3 hours before serving.

SPRING
Sorbet 101

Prep Time: 20 mins
Total Time: 2 hr 20 mins

Servings per Recipe: 6
Calories   125.0
Fat   0.2g
Cholesterol   0.0mg
Sodium   1.5mg
Carbohydrates   31.7g
Protein   0.5g

Ingredients

1 C. water
3/4 C. sugar
1 pint fresh strawberries
1/2 C. orange juice

Directions

1. Combine water & sugar in a pan, stir over low heat until sugar dissolves.
2. Bring to a boil & boil gently for 5 minutes without stirring.
3. Set aside to cool.
4. Wash berries.
5. Remove caps.
6. Puree fruit in a blender or food processor until almost smooth.
7. In a medium bowl, combine fruit with cooled syrup and orange juice.
8. If you have an ice cream freezer, you can put the puree mixture into that & process using the directions
9. In a pan, add the water and sugar on low heat and cook till the sugar dissolves, stirring continuously.
10. Bring to a boil and then boil for about 5 minutes without stirring.
11. Remove from the heat and keep aside to cool.
12. Wash the strawberries and hull them.
13. In a blender, add the strawberries and pulse till smooth.
14. In a bowl, mix together the strawberry puree, cooled sugar syrup and orange juice.
15. Transfer the mixture into ice cream maker and process according to manufacturers

Strawberry Smoothie Bowl

Prep Time: 15 mins
Total Time: 15 mins

Servings per Recipe: 8
Calories	127.2
Fat	5.7g
Cholesterol	20.3mg
Sodium	20.2mg
Carbohydrates	18.4g
Protein	1.6g

Ingredients

500 g strawberries, hulled
2 large egg whites, at room temperature
1/2 C. caster sugar
1/2 C. whipping cream
1/4-1/2 tsp vanilla
6 - 8 strawberries, sliced, for garnish
Mint leaf

Directions

1. In a blender, add the strawberries and pulse till smooth.
2. In a bowl, add the strawberry puree, egg whites and sugar and beat till stiff and glossy.
3. In another bowl, add the cream and vanilla and beat till peaks form.
4. Gently fold the cream mixture into the strawberry mixture.
5. Transfer the mixture into a serving bowl and top with the strawberry slices and mint.
6. With a plastic wrap, cover the bowl and refrigerate before serving.

ALTERNATIVE
Jam

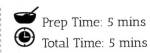

Prep Time: 5 mins
Total Time: 5 mins

Servings per Recipe: 6
Calories	578.4
Fat	1.0g
Cholesterol	0.0mg
Sodium	6.4mg
Carbohydrates	145.8g
Protein	2.4g

Ingredients

2 1/2 C. coarsely chopped hulled
strawberries
1/2 C. sugar
2 1/2 tbsp cornstarch

Directions

1. In a heavy small pan, add all the Ingredients and bring to a boil, crushing the berries slightly with the back of spoon.
2. Now, boil for about 2 minutes, stirring continuously.
3. Transfer the mixture into a bowl and refrigerate to cool completely.

Mid-Summer
Dessert

🍲 Prep Time: 30 mins
🕐 Total Time: 30 mins

Servings per Recipe: 1
Calories	3980.5
Fat	178.4g
Cholesterol	652.1mg
Sodium	4036.6mg
Carbohydrates	558.4g
Protein	61.3g

Ingredients

1 angel food cake
1 (1 lb) container frozen strawberries, with
juice, thawed
1 (6 oz.) packages strawberry Jell-O
gelatin dessert
1 1/4 C. boiling water
1 pint heavy cream, whipped

Directions

1. Tear the angel cake into small pieces and transfer into a bowl.
2. In 1 1/4 C. of the boiling water, dissolve the Jell-O.
3. Add the strawberries and juices and stir to combine.
4. Keep aside to cool completely.
5. After cooling, fold in the whipped cream.
6. Place the strawberry mixture over the angel cake pieces and stir to combine.
7. Transfer the mixture into a bundt pan and refrigerate till firm.
8. Carefully, invert the cake onto a serving platter and cut into desired slices.
9. Serve with a topping of the whipped cream and strawberries.

TRADITIONAL
Pavlova

Prep Time: 30 mins
Total Time: 2 hr

Servings per Recipe: 8
Calories	308.8
Fat	22.2g
Cholesterol	81.5mg
Sodium	44.1mg
Carbohydrates	26.1g
Protein	3.0g

Ingredients

3 egg whites
1 pinch cream of tartar
3/4 C. granulated sugar
1 tsp vanilla
2 C. whipping cream
4 C. strawberries, sliced

Directions

1. Set your oven to 275 degrees F before doing anything else and line a baking sheet with a piece of foil.
2. In a large bowl, add the egg whites and cream of tartar and beat till soft peaks form.
3. Add the sugar, 1 tbsp at a time and beat till glossy peaks form.
4. Add the vanilla and beat till well combined.
5. Place the meringue onto the prepared baking sheet into a 10-inch circle, pushing up the edges to form a slight ridge.
6. Cook in the oven for about 1 1/2 hours.
7. Turn off the oven but leave the meringue in the oven to dry completely.
8. Remove from the oven.
9. Carefully, remove the foil and keep aside to cool completely.
10. Arrange the meringue onto a serving platter.
11. Spread the whipped cream over the meringue and top with the strawberries.
12. Cut into the wedges and serve.

Kansas
Lemonade

Prep Time: 30 mins
Total Time: 30 mins

Servings per Recipe: 6
Calories   171.4
Fat   0.1g
Cholesterol   0.0mg
Sodium   5.3mg
Carbohydrates   45.2g
Protein   0.4g

Ingredients

1 C. lemon juice
1 C. sugar
1 1/2 C. strawberries, washed and hulled
2 tbsp light corn syrup
Water, to fill 2 quart pitcher

Directions

1. In a blender, add the strawberries and corn syrup and pulse till smooth.
2. Through a fine sieve, strain the strawberry puree and discard the pulp and seeds.
3. In a 2 quart pitcher, add the strawberry puree, lemon juice and sugar and mix till the sugar is dissolved.
4. In serving glasses, place the ice.
5. Pour the lemonade over the ice and serve.

LANCASTER
Strawberries

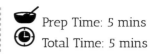
Prep Time: 5 mins
Total Time: 5 mins

Servings per Recipe: 4
Calories	401.0
Fat	41.4g
Cholesterol	144.0mg
Sodium	204.9mg
Carbohydrates	4.0g
Protein	4.5g

Ingredients

8 oz. cream cheese
1 C. whipping cream
1/2 tsp vanilla extract
Strawberry, 1 C. for each serving
Powdered sugar
Mint leaves

Directions

1. In a bowl, add the cream cheese and beat till softened.
2. Slowly, add the cream and beat till the mixture is smooth.
3. Stir in the vanilla extract and powdered sugar.
4. Wash and hull the strawberries and transfer into another bowl.
5. Refrigerate the bowls of strawberries and cream mixture till serving.
6. Divide the strawberries into serving dishes bowls and top with the cream mixture.
7. Serve with a garnishing of the garnish mint leaves.

Strawberry
Party Platter

Prep Time: 10 mins
Total Time: 3 hr 10 mins

Servings per Recipe: 20
Calories	189.9
Fat	12.9g
Cholesterol	28.5mg
Sodium	160.0mg
Carbohydrates	12.6g
Protein	6.5g

Ingredients

16 oz. sharp cheddar cheese, grated
1 (3 oz.) packages cream cheese, softened
3/4 C. mayonnaise
1 small onion, chopped
1 C. chopped pecans
1/2 tsp garlic powder
Cayenne pepper

1 C. strawberry preserves

Directions

1. In a food processor, add all the Ingredients and pulse till well combined.
2. Transfer into a bowl and refrigerate for about 2-3 hours.
3. Now, transfer the mixture onto a platter.
4. With your hands, mold the mixture into a ring formation and top with the strawberry preserves evenly.
5. Serve alongside the buttery crackers.

FRUITY
Cold Soup

Prep Time: 25 mins
Total Time: 25 mins

Servings per Recipe: 1
Calories   299.7
Fat   9.3g
Cholesterol   34.1mg
Sodium   121.2mg
Carbohydrates   47.6g
Protein   8.9g

Ingredients

1 C. strawberry, chopped
1 C. cold milk
2 - 3 tbsp sugar

Directions

1. In a serving bowl, add the strawberries and sprinkle with the sugar.
2. Keep aside for about 10 - 15 minutes.
3. Now, place the milk and mix well.
4. Serve immediately.

Easy
Strawberry Torte

🥘 Prep Time: 20 mins
🕐 Total Time: 50 mins

Servings per Recipe: 12
Calories	375.0
Fat	28.8g
Cholesterol	78.5mg
Sodium	170.3mg
Carbohydrates	27.0g
Protein	3.9g

Ingredients

CRUST
1/2 C. pecans, toasted
1 1/2 C. flour
2 tbsp sugar
3/4 C. cold butter
FILLING
8 oz. cream cheese, room temperature

1/2 C. sugar
1 C. whipping cream
3 C. fresh strawberries, halved

Directions

1. Set your oven to 325 degrees F before doing anything else.
2. In a food processor, add the pecans and pulse till finely chopped.
3. Add the flour and sugar and pulse till well combined.
4. Add the cold butter, 2 tbsp at a time and pulse till well combined.
5. Place the mixture into a spring form pan, pressing the mixture 1-inch up the sides of the pan.
6. Cook in the oven for about 30-40 minutes.
7. Remove from the oven and keep aside to cool.
8. In a bowl, add the cream cheese and sugar and with an electric mixer, beat on high speed till fluffy.
9. While the motor is still running slowly, add the whipping cream in a steady small stream, beating till well combined.
10. Place the cream cheese mixture over the cooled crust evenly.
11. Refrigerate, covered for up to 24 hours.
12. Carefully, remove the torte from the spring form pan and top with the halved strawberries.
13. Cut into desired wedges and serve.

SATURDAY
Night Pudding

Prep Time: 15 mins
Total Time: 35 mins

Servings per Recipe: 8
Calories	153.4
Fat	0.3g
Cholesterol	0.0mg
Sodium	5.4mg
Carbohydrates	38.5g
Protein	0.7g

Ingredients

2 lb. small strawberries
1 C. sugar
1 quart water
1/3 C. cornstarch
1/2 tsp vanilla (optional)
1/2 tsp finely grated lemon zest
(optional)

Directions

1. Clean and rinse the strawberries.
2. In a pan, add the water and bring to a boil on medium heat.
3. Add the sugar and strawberries and simmer for about 8 minutes, breaking the berries with the back of a spoon.
4. Meanwhile in a bowl, add a little water and dissolve the cornstarch.
5. Slowly, add the cornstarch mixture in the pan, stirring continuously.
6. Add the vanilla and lemon zest and bring to a boil, stirring continuously.
7. Boil for a few minutes, stirring continuously.
8. Transfer the mixture into a bowl and refrigerator to cool completely.
9. Serve with a topping of your liking.

How to Make
Strawberry Buckle

Prep Time: 10 mins
Total Time: 10 mins

Servings per Recipe: 10
Calories	312.8
Fat	10.5g
Cholesterol	47.2mg
Sodium	272.4mg
Carbohydrates	51.1g
Protein	4.3g

Ingredients

1/4 C. butter, softened
3/4 C. sugar
1 egg, beaten
1/2 tsp vanilla
1/2 C. milk
2 C. flour, sifted
2 tsp baking powder
1/2 tsp salt

2 C. fresh strawberries, sliced
TOPPING
1/4 C. butter, softened
1/2 C. brown sugar
1/3 C. flour, sifted
1/2 tsp cinnamon
1 dash nutmeg

Directions

1. Set your oven to 375 degrees F before doing anything else and lightly, grease a 9x9-inch baking dish.
2. In a large bowl, add the sugar and butter and beat till light and fluffy.
3. Add the eggs and vanilla and beat till well combined.
4. Add the milk and beat till well combined.
5. In another bowl, sift together the flour, baking powder and salt.
6. Add the egg mixture into the flour mixture and mix till well combined.
7. Fold in the strawberries.
8. Transfer the mixture into the prepared baking dish evenly.
9. For topping in a bowl, add the butter and sugar and beat till creamy.
10. Add the flour and cinnamon and mix well.
11. Spread the flour mixture over the strawberry mixture evenly and sprinkle with the nutmeg.
12. Cook in the oven for about 30-35 minutes.
13. Serve warm with the topping of the cream.

STRAWBERRY
Cobbler

Prep Time: 10 mins
Total Time: 1 hr

Servings per Recipe: 4
Calories	473.2
Fat	13.4g
Cholesterol	77.0mg
Sodium	167.0mg
Carbohydrates	85.1g
Protein	5.8g

Ingredients

4 C. strawberries, cleaned and sliced
1 C. all-purpose flour
1/2 tsp baking powder
1 C. sugar
1 egg, beaten
1/4 C. butter, in cubes

Directions

1. Set your oven to 375 degrees F before doing anything else.
2. In a bowl, mix together the flour, baking powder and sugar.
3. Add the egg and with a fork, mix till a crumbly mixture forms.
4. In the bottom of a 9-inch square baking dish, place the strawberries and top with the flour mixture evenly.
5. Place the butter on top in the form of the dots.
6. Cook in the oven for about 45-50 minutes.
7. Remove from the oven and keep on wire rack to cool slightly.
8. Serve warm.

Lolly
Strawberries

Prep Time: 5 mins
Total Time: 5 mins

Servings per Recipe: 4

Calories	89.1
Fat	2.9g
Cholesterol	5.2mg
Sodium	9.5mg
Carbohydrates	16.0g
Protein	1.3g

Ingredients

4 C. fresh strawberries
4 tbsp sour cream
4 tsp brown sugar

Directions

1. Wash, hull and drain the strawberries completely.
2. Divide the strawberries in 4 dessert bowls and top with the sour cream evenly.
3. Serve with a sprinkling of the brown sugar.

STRAWBERRY CAKE
with No-Bake

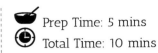 Prep Time: 5 mins
Total Time: 10 mins

Servings per Recipe: 2
Calories	420.5
Fat	14.6g
Cholesterol	0.7mg
Sodium	46.9mg
Carbohydrates	73.8g
Protein	5.2g

Ingredients

4 C. strawberries, frozen, halved
1/2 C. coconut cream
2 C. pineapple juice, chilled
1/2 C. crushed pineapple
2 tsp whipped cream
2 large strawberries
1 tsp white sugar

Directions

1. In a food processor, add the strawberries, coconut cream, pineapple juice and crushed pineapple and pulse till smooth.
2. Divide the strawberry mixture into 2 chilled glasses.
3. Place the dollop of the whipped cream in the center of each glass and arrange 1 strawberry beside the whipped cream.
4. Serve with a sprinkling of the sugar.

Mountain-Time Strawberries

Prep Time: 2 mins
Total Time: 4 mins

Servings per Recipe: 4
Calories	27.2
Fat	0.1g
Cholesterol	0.0mg
Sodium	1.3mg
Carbohydrates	6.6g
Protein	0.2g

Ingredients

8 large strawberries, whole & cleaned
1 tbsp balsamic vinegar
1 tbsp sugar

Directions

1. Set your grill for high heat and lightly, grease the grill grate.
2. Dip the strawberries in the balsamic vinegar evenly and then coat with the sugar.
3. Cook the strawberries on the grill for about 1-2 minutes.
4. Remove from the grill and serve immediately.

STRAWBERRY
Mousse

Prep Time: 30 mins
Total Time: 30 mins

Servings per Recipe: 4
Calories	375.7
Fat	27.8g
Cholesterol	101.8mg
Sodium	29.7mg
Carbohydrates	32.0g
Protein	2.2g

Ingredients

1 lb ripe strawberry, hulled and sliced
2 tbsp granulated sugar
1 tbsp kirsch
1/2 C. confectioners' sugar
1 1/4 C. heavy cream

Directions

1. In a bowl, add half of the strawberries and sprinkle with the granulated sugar and kirsch.
2. Keep aside for about 15 minutes.
3. In a blender, add the remaining strawberries and confectioners' sugar and pulse till smooth.
4. In another bowl, add the cream and beat till stiff peaks form.
5. In a small bowl, add 1/4 of the whipped cream reserve for the garnishing in refrigerator.
6. Gently, fold the remaining cream into the strawberries puree.
7. Divide the strawberry mixture in 4 balloon-shaped wine glasses, reserving a few strawberry slices for garnish.
8. Fill each glass with the strawberry cream evenly.
9. With the plastic wraps, cover the glasses and refrigerate for a few hours.
10. Place the reserved whipped cream in a pastry bag, fitted with a star tip and decorate the mousse.
11. Serve with a garnishing of the remaining strawberries slices.

French
Toast 101

🥣 Prep Time: 10 mins
🕐 Total Time: 20 mins

Servings per Recipe: 4
Calories	449.9
Fat	26.3g
Cholesterol	158.1mg
Sodium	476.4mg
Carbohydrates	44.7g
Protein	9.2g

Ingredients

1 (3 oz.) packages cream cheese, softened
2 tbsp confectioners' sugar
2 tbsp strawberry preserves
8 slices country white bread
2 eggs
1/2 C. half-and-half
2 tbsp granulated sugar
4 tbsp butter

Directions

1. In a small bowl, add the cream cheese and confectioners' sugar and mix well.
2. Add the strawberry preserves and mix well.
3. Place the cream cheese mixture over 4 bread slices evenly and cover with the remaining bread slices to form the sandwiches.
4. In a shallow bowl, add the eggs, half-and-half and granulated sugar and beat till well combined.
5. Dip each sandwich in the egg mixture evenly.
6. In a large skillet, melt 2 tbsp of the butter on medium heat and cook 2 sandwiches for about 1-2 minutes per side.
7. Repeat with the remaining butter and sandwiches.
8. Slice the sandwiches in half diagonally and serve immediately.

APRICOTS, HONEY
and Squash
Tagine

Prep Time: 45 mins
Total Time: 2 hr 45 mins

Servings per Recipe: 4
Calories   540.3
Cholesterol   120.0mg
Sodium   572.7mg
Carbohydrates   43.2g
Protein   34.8g

Ingredients

2 lbs cubed lamb
1 tbsp vegetable oil
1 large onion, diced
1 1/2 C. water
1 pinch saffron thread, crumbled
3/4 tsp salt
1/4 tsp black pepper
1 1/2 large carrots, cut into 1/4-inch-thick rounds
1 small sweet potato, skin removed and

cut into 3/4-inch pieces
3/4 tsp ground ginger
1/8 tsp cinnamon
2/3 C. pitted prune
1/2 C. dried apricot
1 medium yellow squash, cut into 3/4-inch pieces
2 tsps honey
freshly grated nutmeg

Directions

1. Sear half of your meat in 1/2 tsp of oil then place it to the side then sear the rest of the meat.
2. Add half a tsp more of oil to the tagine and begin to stir fry your onions until they are tender then add the meat back in.
3. Also add in the pepper, salt, saffron, and water.
4. Get everything boiling, set the heat to low, and place a lid on the tagine.
5. Let the mix cook for 90 mins then place the lamb on a serving dish.
6. Add the sweet potatoes and carrots to the tagine and cook the veggies, with the lid on the pot, for 12 mins then stir in the squash, ginger, apricots, cinnamon, and prunes.
7. Continue cooking the new veggies for 7 mins then add the meat back in also the honey.
8. Stir the honey into the tagine then add the nutmeg, more pepper, and more salt.
9. Let the tagine cook for 7 more mins with no lid.
10. Enjoy.

Apricot Sweet Delicacy

🥄 Prep Time: 10 mins
🕐 Total Time: 40 mins

Servings per Recipe: 24
Calories   141 kcal
Fat   6.5 g
Carbohydrates   20.1g
Protein   2.2 g
Cholesterol   23 mg
Sodium   54 mg

Ingredients

3 eggs
1/2 C. white sugar
3/4 C. chopped walnuts
2 C. flaked coconut
7 1/2 oz. vanilla wafers, crushed
8 oz. dried apricots

Directions

1. Cut the apricots into small strips and place in in a sealed container.
2. Drizzle with the water and keep aside for overnight.
3. In a bowl, mix together the eggs, sugar and apricots.
4. Heat a lightly buttered skillet on low heat and cook the apricot mixture for about 10 minutes.
5. Stir in the walnuts, vanilla wafer crumbs and 1/2 of the coconut.
6. Make small equal sized balls from the mixture and roll in the remaining coconut.
7. Store in a tightly covered box.

I ♥ APRICOT
Fruitcake

🥣 Prep Time: 20 mins
🕐 Total Time: 2 hr 20 mins

Servings per Recipe: 24
Calories	296 kcal
Fat	10 g
Carbohydrates	51g
Protein	3.8 g
Cholesterol	46 mg
Sodium	145 mg

Ingredients

1 C. dried apricots
1 C. water
3/4 C. butter
1 C. white sugar
4 eggs, separated
1 C. golden raisins
1 lb. red and green candied cherries
6 candied pineapple slices
1 lb. dried mixed fruit
2 C. all-purpose flour, divided
1/2 tsp baking soda
1/2 tsp salt
1/2 C. apricot nectar
1 C. chopped walnuts

Directions

1. Set your oven to 275 degrees F before doing anything else and grease 2 (9-inch) tube pans.
2. In a pan, add the apricots and water on medium heat and cook till they are mushy.
3. Through a sieve, strain the apricots by pressing and keep aside to cool.
4. In a small bowl, add the egg yolks and beat till lemony colored.
5. In another small bowl, add the egg whites and beat till stiff peaks formed.
6. In a large bowl, add the butter and sugar and beat till creamy.
7. Add the beaten egg yolks and the apricots and mix till well combined.
8. In a second bowl, mix together 1 C. of the flour, raisins, candied cherries, candied pineapple and mixed dried fruits.
9. In a third bowl, mix together the remaining flour, baking soda and salt.
10. Add the flour mixture alternately to the creamed mixture with the apricot nectar and mix till well combined.
11. Add the flour mixture and walnuts into the mixed fruit mixture and mix till well combined.
12. Fold in the beaten egg whites.
13. Divide the mixture into the prepared pans evenly.
14. Cook in the oven for about 2 hours.
15. Serve these cakes with a garnishing of the candied pineapples and cherries.

Oven Roasted
Apricots

Prep Time: 10 mins
Total Time: 1 hr 10 mins

Servings per Recipe: 6
Calories	588 kcal
Fat	21.7 g
Carbohydrates	100g
Protein	3.4 g
Cholesterol	62 mg
Sodium	342 mg

Ingredients

3 (15 oz.) cans apricot halves, drained
3/4 C. packed brown sugar
50 buttery round crackers, crumbled
1/2 C. butter, melted

Directions

1. Set your oven to 325 degrees F before doing anything else.
2. In the bottom of 12x8-inch baking dish place a layer of 1/2 of the apricots, followed by the brown sugar, cracker crumbs and butter.
3. Repeat the layer once.
4. Cook in the oven for about 50-60 minutes.

FRESH
Summer Salsa

Prep Time: 40 mins
Total Time: 2 hr 40 mins

Servings per Recipe: 15
Calories	30 kcal
Fat	0.2 g
Carbohydrates	< 7.1g
Protein	0.9 g
Cholesterol	0 mg
Sodium	3 mg

Ingredients

3 C. chopped fresh apricot
1 C. shallots, julienned
1/2 C. chopped green bell pepper
1/2 C. chopped red bell pepper
1/2 C. chopped fresh pineapple
1/4 C. chopped cherry tomatoes
1 habanero pepper, seeded and minced

2 cloves garlic, minced
1 tsp minced fresh cilantro
1/2 tsp cumin
1/4 C. fresh lime juice

Directions

1. In a large bowl, mix together all the ingredients.
2. Refrigerate for at least 2 hours before serving.

South Asian
Inspired Chutney

🥣 Prep Time: 15 mins
🕐 Total Time: 1 hr 20 mins

Servings per Recipe: 50	
Calories	51 kcal
Fat	0.3 g
Carbohydrates	< 12.9 g
Protein	0.2 g
Cholesterol	< 0 mg
Sodium	31 mg

Ingredients

1/2 whole head garlic
1/4 tsp olive oil
1 large onion, chopped
1 tbsp olive oil
3 C. apricot preserves
1 C. white vinegar
2 tsp ground ginger

1/2 tsp cayenne pepper
1/2 tsp salt

Directions

1. Set your oven to 450 degrees F before doing anything else.
2. With a sharp knife, cut the top off the half head of garlic, exposing the cloves and discard the top.
3. Place the head of garlic on a piece of the foil and drizzle with 1/4 tsp of the olive oil.
4. Wrap the foil around the garlic.
5. Cook in the oven for about 30 - 40 minutes.
6. Meanwhile in a pan, add the onion and 1 tbsp of the olive oil on medium heat and cook for about 10 - 15 minutes.
7. Remove from the heat and add the apricot preserves, vinegar, ginger, cayenne pepper and salt and stir till well combined.
8. Squeeze the roasted garlic cloves out of their skins and pace into a bowl.
9. With a spoon, mash the garlic cloves.
10. Add the garlic into the chutney and bring to a boil on medium heat.
11. Reduce the heat and simmer for about 25 minutes, stirring occasionally.
12. Transfer the chutney into sterilized jars and process to seal.

MIDSUMMER'S
Night Pie

Prep Time: 25 mins
Total Time: 2 hr

Servings per Recipe: 8

Calories	542 kcal
Fat	27.6 g
Carbohydrates	69.9g
Protein	5.9 g
Cholesterol	0 mg
Sodium	293 mg

Ingredients

2 1/2 C. all-purpose flour
1 tsp salt
1 C. butter-flavored shortening
6 tbsp water
1 C. white sugar
1/4 C. all-purpose flour
1/4 tsp ground cinnamon

1 tsp lemon juice
5 C. fresh apricots, pitted and quartered
1 tsp sugar for sprinkling

Directions

1. Set your oven to 425 degrees F before doing anything else and arrange the rack in the center of the oven.
2. In a bowl, mix together 2 1/2 C. of the flour and the salt.
3. With a pastry cutter, cut the shortening into the flour mixture till the mixture is crumbly.
4. Add the water, 1 tbsp at a time and with a fork, mix till the dough just holds together.
5. Divide the dough in 2 equal portions and form each portion into a ball.
6. Place each ball onto a floured surface and roll each ball out into a crust big enough for a 9-inch pie dish.
7. Carefully lift a crust and fold into quarters.
8. Arrange into a pie dish and unfold the crust.
9. Keep the other crust aside.
10. In a large bowl, add the sugar, 1/4 C. of the flour and cinnamon and mix till well combined.
11. Stir in the lemon juice and apricots.
12. Place the mixture over the pie crust and top with the reserved crust.
13. With a fork, crimp the edges of the crusts together and cut away the excess crust.
14. Carefully, cut the slits into the pie to allow steam to escape.
15. With the strips of foil, cover the edges of the pie crust to prevent burning.
16. Cook in the oven for about 35-45 minutes.
17. Remove from the oven and keep onto a rack to cool.
18. Sprinkle the top with 1 tsp of the sugar.

Sunday's
Beef Brisket

Prep Time: 15 mins
Total Time: 3 hr 45 mins

Servings per Recipe: 6
Calories	822 kcal
Fat	43.8 g
Carbohydrates	52.4g
Protein	56.3 g
Cholesterol	185 mg
Sodium	550 mg

Ingredients

2 tbsp vegetable oil
6 lb. beef brisket
1 onion, chopped
2 cloves crushed garlic
1 (1 oz.) package dry onion soup mix
1 lb. dried apricots

Directions

1. Set your oven to 325 degrees F before doing anything.
2. In a large heavy skillet, heat the oil on medium-high heat and cook the brisket till browned from all sides.
3. Transfer the brisket in a large Dutch oven.
4. Add the onions into the drippings in the skillet on medium heat and sauté till the onions are beginning to brown.
5. Stir in the garlic and sauté for about 2-3 minutes.
6. Place the onion mixture over the brisket in the Dutch oven.
7. Place 1 package of dry, instant onion soup mix over the browned onions and brisket.
8. Place the apricots on top of the soup mix and add enough water to cover the sides of brisket.
9. Cook in the oven, covered for about 1 hour.
10. Add a bit more water around meat and cook, covered for about 1 hour.
11. Uncover and stir apricots into gravy and cook for about 1 hour.
12. Stir gravy again, and add more water if the gravy is too thick.
13. Cook for about 1/2 hour more.
14. Cut the brisket across grain and serve.

CENTRAL
European Dumplings

 Prep Time: 10 mins
Total Time: 40 mins

Servings per Recipe: 6

Calories	689 kcal
Fat	15.4 g
Carbohydrates	137.6g
Protein	5.6 g
Cholesterol	31 mg
Sodium	548 mg

Ingredients

5 C. fresh apricots, pitted and sliced
3 C. water
3 C. white sugar
6 tbsp butter
2 tbsp lemon juice
1/2 tsp salt
8 (6 inch) flour tortillas

Directions

1. In a large pan, mix together the apricots, water, sugar, lemon juice, salt and butter on medium-low heat and cook till the apricots are cooked completely.
2. Cut the tortillas into 1-inch strips.
3. Reduce the heat to low.
4. Add the tortilla strips, a few at a time into the pan with apricots and cook for about 20 minutes.

Apricot
Swirls

Prep Time: 20 mins
Total Time: 1 hr 30 mins

Servings per Recipe: 24
Calories	109 kcal
Fat	5.9 g
Carbohydrates	13g
Protein	1.2 g
Cholesterol	15 mg
Sodium	97 mg

Ingredients

2 C. all-purpose flour
1/3 C. white sugar
1/2 tsp salt
1/2 tsp ground mace
1/4 tsp baking powder
3/4 C. butter
6 tbsp water

1/4 tsp lemon extract
1/4 C. apricot preserves
3 tbsp milk

Directions

1. In a bowl, mix together the flour, sugar, salt, mace and baking powder.
2. With a pastry cutter, cut the butter till the mixture resembles coarse crumbs.
3. Add 1 tbsp of the water and lemon extract and with a fork, gently mix.
4. Repeat with the remaining cold water, 1 tbsp at a time.
5. Make a ball from the mixture.
6. Cover the ball refrigerate to chill for about 30 minutes.
7. Set your oven to 375 degrees F.
8. Divide the dough into 4 equal sized portions.
9. Roll 2 portions into 12x4-inch rectangles.
10. Spread the preserves over 2 rolled rectangles.
11. Roll the remaining 2 portions into 12x4-inch rectangles and carefully place over those spread with the preserves.
12. Trim the edges and cut each rectangle into twelve 4x1-inch strips.
13. Twist each strip twice and pinch ends to seal.
14. Arrange the strips onto an ungreased cookie sheet.
15. Cook in the oven for about 15 minutes.
16. Remove from the oven and coat with the milk.
17. Sprinkle with the additional sugar and cook in the oven for about 5-8 minutes more.
18. Remove from the oven and cool on wire rack.

APRICOT
Spread

Prep Time: 20 mins
Total Time: 2 hr

Servings per Recipe: 50
Calories	105 kcal
Fat	0.1 g
Carbohydrates	< 26.9g
Protein	0.4 g
Cholesterol	< 0 mg
Sodium	< 1 mg

Ingredients

8 C. fresh apricots - peeled, pitted, and
crushed
1/4 C. lemon juice
6 C. white sugar
5 (1 pint) canning jars with lids and
rings

Directions

1. In a large pan, mix together the apricots and lemon juice and slowly bring to a boil, stirring continuously till the sugar is dissolved.
2. Cook for about 25 minutes, stirring occasionally.
3. Remove from the heat and skim the foam if desired.
4. Meanwhile, prepare jars, lids, and rings by cleaning and sterilizing in boiling water bath.
5. Leave lids in simmering water before sealing the jars.
6. Ladle hot jam into hot sterilized jars, leaving about 1/4-inch of space on top.
7. Run a knife around the insides of the jars to remove any air bubbles.
8. With a moist paper towel, wipe the rims of the jars to remove any food residue.
9. Top with the lids and screw on rings.
10. Place a rack in the bottom of a large pan and fill halfway with the water.
11. Bring to a boil and carefully with a holder, lower the jars into the pan, leaving a 2-inch space between the jars.
12. Bring the water to a full boil and process, covered for 15 minutes.
13. Remove the jars from the pan and place onto a cloth-covered surface, several inches apart to cool.
14. After cooling with a finger, press the top of each lid, ensuring that the seal is tight.
15. Store in a cool, dark area.

Potluck
Dessert Salad

Prep Time: 10 mins
Total Time: 1 hr 10 mins

Servings per Recipe: 18
Calories   256 kcal
Fat   10.9 g
Carbohydrates   37.8g
Protein   4 g
Cholesterol   21 mg
Sodium   103 mg

Ingredients

1 (6 oz.) package apricot flavored Jell-O(R) mix
2/3 C. white sugar
2/3 C. water
2 (4 oz.) jars apricot baby food
1 (20 oz.) can crushed pineapple with juice

1 (8 oz.) package cream cheese, softened
1 (14 oz.) can sweetened condensed milk
1/3 C. chopped pecans
1 (8 oz.) container frozen whipped topping, thawed

Directions

1. In a small pan, mix together the gelatin, sugar and water and bring to a boil, stirring till dissolved completely.
2. Remove from the heat and stir in the baby food and pineapple with the juice.
3. Keep aside to cool for about 10 minutes.
4. In a small bowl, add the cream cheese and sweetened condensed milk and mix till smooth.
5. Add the cream cheese mixture into the pineapple mixture and beat till combined.
6. Stir in the pecans and transfer the mixture into a 13x9-inch baking dish.
7. Refrigerate to chill completely.
8. Top with the thawed whipped topping and sprinkle with the extra pecans.
9. Cut into desired size squares.

WHIPPED WINTER
Apricots

Prep Time: 15 mins
Total Time: 3 hr 15 mins

Servings per Recipe: 12
Calories	250 kcal
Fat	12.9 g
Carbohydrates	32.7g
Protein	3.2 g
Cholesterol	17 mg
Sodium	79 mg

Ingredients

1 quart apricot nectar
2 (3 oz.) packages apricot flavored Jell-O(R) mix
1 pint sour cream
1 (8.75 oz.) can apricot halves, drained and chopped
1 (8 oz.) tub frozen whipped topping, thawed

Directions

1. In a pan, add the apricot nectar and bring to a boil.
2. Remove from the heat.
3. Immediately, add the gelatin mix and stir till dissolved completely.
4. Add the sour cream and beat till smooth.
5. Transfer the mixture into a serving bowl and stir in the apricots.
6. Refrigerate to set for about 3 hours.
7. Serve with a topping of the whipped topping.

Classical
Fruit Squares

Prep Time: 30 mins
Total Time: 1 hr 15 mins

Servings per Recipe: 32

Calories	105 kcal
Fat	4.4 g
Carbohydrates	15.5g
Protein	1.3 g
Cholesterol	19 mg
Sodium	53 mg

Ingredients

2/3 C. dried apricots
1/2 C. butter, softened
1/4 C. white sugar
1 C. sifted all-purpose flour
2 eggs
1 C. packed brown sugar
1/3 C. sifted all-purpose flour

1/2 tsp baking powder
1/4 tsp salt
1/2 tsp vanilla extract
1/2 C. chopped walnuts
1/3 C. confectioners' sugar for decoration

Directions

1. Set your oven to 350 degrees F before doing anything else and grease an 8x8-inch square baking dish.
2. In a small pan, add the apricots and enough water to cover on medium heat and bring to a boil.
3. Boil for about 10 minutes.
4. Drain completely and keep aside to cool.
5. After cooling, chop the apricots roughly.
6. In a bowl, add the butter, 1/4 C. of the sugar and 1 C. of the flour and mix till crumbly.
7. Spread the crumbly mixture into the prepared baking dish evenly and press to smooth.
8. Cook in the oven for about 20-25 minutes.
9. In a large bowl, add the eggs and brown sugar and beat till well combined.
10. In another bowl, mix together 1/3 C. of the flour, baking powder and salt.
11. Add the flour mixture into the egg mixture and stir to combine.
12. Fold in the vanilla, walnuts and apricots.
13. Place the mixture over the baked layer evenly.
14. Cook in the oven for about 20-25 minutes.
15. Remove from the oven and cool on wire racks.
16. Cut into bars and coat with the confectioner's sugar before serving.

TUESDAY
Breakfast Muffins

Prep Time: 15 mins
Total Time: 30 mins

Servings per Recipe: 12

Calories	238 kcal
Fat	9.2 g
Carbohydrates	36.2g
Protein	3.8 g
Cholesterol	26 mg
Sodium	258 mg

Ingredients

1 C. chopped dried apricots
1 C. boiling water
2 C. all-purpose flour
3/4 C. white sugar
1 tsp baking soda
1/2 tsp salt
1/4 C. melted butter

1/4 C. vegetable oil
1 C. buttermilk
1 egg

Directions

1. Set your oven to 400 degrees F before doing anything else and grease 12 cups of a muffin pan.
2. In a bowl, add the apricots and boiling water and keep aside for about 5 minutes.
3. Drain the apricots completely.
4. In a bowl, mix together the flour, sugar, baking soda and salt.
5. In another bowl, add the melted butter, oil, buttermilk and egg and beat till well combined.
6. Add the egg mixture into the flour mixture and mix till just moistened.
7. Fold in the apricots.
8. Transfer the mixture into the prepared muffin cups evenly.
9. Cook in the oven for about 15 minutes or till a toothpick inserted in the center comes out clean.
10. Remove from the oven and place on wire rack to cool completely.

Teatime
Every Time Cookies

Prep Time: 10 mins
Total Time: 1 hr

Servings per Recipe: 24

Calories	202 kcal
Fat	8 g
Carbohydrates	31.2g
Protein	2 g
Cholesterol	28 mg
Sodium	127 mg

Ingredients

1 C. butter
1 C. white sugar
3 C. all-purpose flour
1 tsp baking powder
1/2 tsp salt
1 egg
1 tsp vanilla extract

1 C. apricot preserves
1/3 C. confectioners' sugar for decoration

Directions

1. Set your oven to 350 degrees F before doing anything.
2. In a bowl, add the butter and sugar and beat till creamy.
3. Add the flour, baking powder, salt, egg and vanilla extract and mix till a dough forms.
4. Refrigerator the dough for about 1 hour.
5. Place the dough onto a lightly floured surface and roll into 1/4-inch thickness.
6. With a round cookie cutter, cut the dough into rounds.
7. With the tip of a tsp, place a small drop of apricot preserves into the center of each round and brush the edges with the water.
8. Fold the dough over so that the cookies change in the shape of a half moon.
9. Seal the edges and place onto an ungreased cookie sheets.
10. Cook in the oven for about 8-12 minutes.
11. Dust the hot cookies with the powdered sugar.

APRICOT
Confetti Cookies

Prep Time: 20 mins
Total Time: 1 hr

Servings per Recipe: 12
Calories	480 kcal
Fat	24.6 g
Carbohydrates	60.7g
Protein	6.3 g
Cholesterol	31 mg
Sodium	94 mg

Ingredients

1 C. chopped walnuts
3 1/2 C. all-purpose flour
3/4 C. white sugar
2 tsp baking powder
2 eggs
1 C. shortening
1 C. apricot preserves

2 tsp ground cinnamon

Directions

1. Set your oven to 350 degrees F before doing anything else.
2. In a large bowl, add the sugar, eggs and shortening and with your hands mix well.
3. Add flour and baking powder and mix till a dough forms.
4. Divide the dough in 2 equal sized portions.
5. In a 15x10-inch baking dish, place 1 dough portion evenly.
6. Spread the preserves over the dough evenly.
7. Spread the walnuts on top and sprinkle with the cinnamon evenly.
8. Crumble the second dough portion on top and gently, press down.
9. Cook in the oven for about 30 minutes.
10. Remove from the oven and place on wire rack to cool completely.
11. After cooling, cut into squares and serve.

Traditional
Czech Cookies

Prep Time: 20 mins
Total Time: 1 hr 20 mins

Servings per Recipe: 6
Calories	674 kcal
Fat	41.1 g
Carbohydrates	71.9g
Protein	7.3 g
Cholesterol	113 mg
Sodium	304 mg

Ingredients

1 C. butter, softened
6 oz. cream cheese, softened
2 tbsp white sugar
2 C. all-purpose flour
3/4 C. dried apricots
1 1/2 C. water
3/4 C. white sugar

Directions

1. For filling in a heavy pan, mix together the apricots and water on medium heat and cook, covered for about 10 minutes.
2. Uncover and cook for about 5-10 minutes or till most of the water is absorbed.
3. Remove from the heat ad with a potato masher, mash the apricots.
4. Stir in 2 tbsp of the sugar and keep aside to cool.
5. For dough in a bowl, add the butter and cream cheese and fluffy.
6. Add 3/4 C. of the sugar and beat well.
7. Add the flour and mix till a dough forms.
8. Make a ball from the dough and refrigerate to chill for about 1 hour.
9. Set your oven to 400 degrees F.
10. Divide the dough into 2 equal sized portions.
11. Place each portion of the dough onto well-floured surface and roll into 1/8-inch thickness.
12. Cut the rolled dough portions into 2-inch squares.
13. Place about 1/2 tsp of apricot filling in the center of each square.
14. Bring four corners to center and pinch to seal.
15. Cook in the oven for about 15 minutes.
16. Serve with a sprinkling of the powdered sugar.

CORPORATE CHRISTMAS
Party Cookies

Prep Time: 15 mins
Total Time: 2 hr 30 mins

Servings per Recipe: 84	
Calories	89 kcal
Fat	4.4 g
Carbohydrates	11.8g
Protein	1.1 g
Cholesterol	16 mg
Sodium	43 mg

Ingredients

1 1/2 C. butter, softened
1 1/2 C. white sugar
1 (8 oz.) package cream cheese, softened
2 eggs
2 tbsp lemon juice
1 1/2 tsp lemon zest

4 1/2 C. all-purpose flour
1 1/2 tsp baking powder
1 C. apricot preserves
1/3 C. confectioners' sugar for decoration

Directions

1. In a large bowl, add the butter, sugar and cream cheese and beat till smooth.
2. Add the eggs, one at a time and beat till well combined.
3. Stir in the lemon juice and lemon zest.
4. Add the flour and baking powder and stir till just combined.
5. Refrigerate, covered for about 1 hour.
6. Set your oven to 350 degrees F.
7. Roll tbsps of the dough into balls, and place onto ungreased cookie sheets about 2-inch apart.
8. With your finger, make an indention in the center of each ball and fill with 1/2 tsp of the apricot preserves.
9. Cook in the oven for about 15 minutes.
10. Remove from the oven and cool the cookies on the cookie sheet for about 2 minutes before removing to wire racks to cool completely.
11. Serve with a sprinkling of the confectioner's sugar.

Apricots
Dessert Rollies

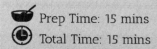

Prep Time: 15 mins
Total Time: 15 mins

Servings per Recipe: 12

Calories	210 kcal
Fat	9 g
Carbohydrates	32.5g
Protein	2.7 g
Cholesterol	6 mg
Sodium	30 mg

Ingredients

1/2 lb. dried apricots
1/2 C. brown sugar
1/2 C. flaked coconut
1/2 (14 oz.) can sweetened condensed milk
1 C. flaked coconut for rolling

Directions

1. In a food processor, add the apricots and pulse till minced.
2. In a bowl, add the minced apricots and brown sugar and toss to coat well.
3. In a shallow dish, mix together 1/2 C. of the coconut and condensed milk.
4. Make 1-inch balls from the apricot mixture and coat with the coconut mixture.
5. Refrigerate before serving.

MOROCCAN
Rice Tagine

Prep Time: 5 mins
Total Time: 40 mins

Servings per Recipe: 6
Calories   426.0
Cholesterol   46.8mg
Sodium   316.2mg
Carbohydrates   55.7g
Protein   24.7g

Ingredients

2 tsps vegetable oil
1 onion, diced
3 garlic cloves, minced
1 lb extra lean ground beef
3/4 tsp allspice
3/4 tsp cinnamon
1 C. brown rice

2 C. chicken broth
1 sweet red pepper, diced
1 yellow pepper, diced
1 C. dried apricots
3 tbsps minced of fresh mint
2 tbsps fresh lemon juice
1/2 C. raw sunflower seeds

Directions

1. Begin to stir fry your garlic and onions in a Dutch oven for 2 mins then add in the beef and cook the meat for 7 mins while breaking it into pieces with a large spoon.
2. Now add the broth, rice, allspice and cinnamon.
3. Stir the spices into the broth and get everything boiling.
4. Place a lid on the pot and let the mix gently boil, with a medium level of heat, for 42 mins.
5. Once the rice is done add in the lemon juice, sweet peppers, mint, and dried fruit.
6. Shut the heat and garnish each serving with sunflower.
7. Enjoy.

Southern
Fried Pies

Prep Time: 30 mins
Total Time: 30 mins

Servings per Recipe: 18
Calories	280 kcal
Fat	14.4 g
Carbohydrates	34.8g
Protein	3.6 g
Cholesterol	1 mg
Sodium	< 266 mg

Ingredients

Dough:
4 C. all-purpose flour
2 tsp salt
1 C. shortening
1 C. milk
Filling:
8 oz. dried apricots

1 (6 oz.) package dried peaches
3/4 C. white sugar
water to cover
2 C. vegetable oil for frying

Directions

1. For crust in a large bowl, mix together the flour and salt.
2. With a pastry cutter, cut the shortening till the mixture is crumbly.
3. Add the milk and mix till the dough forms a ball.
4. Roll the dough and cut into 18 (6-inch) circles and keep aside.
5. For filling in a large pan, add the apricots, peaches and sugar and enough water to cover on low heat and cook, covered till the fruit is falling apart.
6. Uncover and cook till the water is absorbed.
7. In small high-sided skillet, heat the oil medium heat.
8. Place the equal amounts of filling into each pastry circle and fold in half.
9. Seal the pies with a fork dipped in cold water.
10. Fry the pies in batches till browned from all sides.
11. Transfer the pies onto paper towel lined plate to drain.

NORTHERN AFRICAN
Soup

Prep Time: 15 mins
Total Time: 1 hr 5 mins

Servings per Recipe: 6
Calories	263 kcal
Fat	7.4 g
Carbohydrates	37.2g
Protein	13.2 g
Cholesterol	0 mg
Sodium	7 mg

Ingredients

3 tbsp olive oil
1 onion, chopped
2 cloves garlic, minced
1/3 C. dried apricots
1 1/2 C. red lentils
5 C. chicken stock
3 roma (plum) tomatoes - peeled,

seeded and chopped
1/2 tsp ground cumin
1/2 tsp dried thyme
salt to taste
ground black pepper to taste
2 tbsp fresh lemon juice

Directions

1. In a pan, heat the olive oil and sauté the onion, garlic and apricots till tender.
2. Add the lentils and stock and bring to a boil.
3. Reduce the heat and simmer for about 30 minutes.
4. Stir in the tomatoes, cumin, thyme, salt and pepper and simmer for about 10 minutes.
5. Stir in the lemon juice and remove from the heat.
6. In a blender, add 1/2 of the soup and pulse till smooth.
7. Return the pureed soup into the pan and stir with remaining hot soup.
8. Serve immediately.

How to Make
a Coffee Cake

Prep Time: 20 mins
Total Time: 50 mins

Servings per Recipe: 15

Calories	334 kcal
Fat	17.4 g
Carbohydrates	40.2g
Protein	5.6 g
Cholesterol	66 mg
Sodium	304 mg

Ingredients

1 (18.25 oz.) package white cake mix
3 eggs
1 1/2 C. sour cream
1 (15 oz.) can apricot halves, drained
1 tbsp butter
1/2 C. slivered almonds
1 (8 oz.) package cream cheese

2 tbsp milk
2/3 C. confectioners' sugar
2 tsp water

Directions

1. Set your oven to 350 degrees F before doing anything else and grease and flour a 15x10-inch jellyroll pan.
2. Reserve about 1/2 C. of the dry cake mix.
3. In a bowl, add the eggs and sour cream and beat till well combined.
4. Add the remaining cake mix and mix till a lumpy mixture forms.
5. Transfer the mixture into the prepared pan evenly.
6. With the back of a spoon, make 15 wells in the mixture, 3 rows of 5.
7. In another bowl, add the cream cheese and milk and beat till fluffy.
8. Place one tbsp of the cream cheese mixture into each well.
9. Place 1 apricot half, cut side up over each blob of cream cheese.
10. In a small bowl, mix together the reserved cake mix and butter.
11. Add the butter and mix till the mixture becomes crumbly.
12. Fold in the slivered almonds.
13. Sprinkle the mixture over the Danish evenly.
14. Cook in the oven for about 30-35 minutes or till a toothpick inserted in the center comes out clean.
15. For the glaze, in a bowl, add the confectioners' sugar and water and mix till smooth.
16. Drizzle the glaze over the Danish after cooling.

TRADITIONAL
Jewish Pastries (Rugelach)

 Prep Time: 10 mins
Total Time: 1 hr 20 mins

Servings per Recipe: 48
Calories   116 kcal
Fat   7.1 g
Carbohydrates   12.3g
Protein   1.4 g
Cholesterol   15 mg
Sodium   54 mg

Ingredients

1 C. butter, softened
1 (8 oz.) package cream cheese, softened
1 tsp vanilla extract
1/4 tsp salt
2 C. all-purpose flour
3/4 C. white sugar
1 C. chopped walnuts
3/4 C. dried apricots, chopped
1/4 C. packed brown sugar
1 1/2 tsp ground cinnamon
1/2 C. seedless raspberry preserves
1 tbsp milk

Directions

1. In large bowl, add the butter and cream cheese and with mixer at low speed, beat till smooth.
2. Add the vanilla extract, salt, 1 C. of the flour and 1/4 C. of the sugar and beat till well combined.
3. Stir in the remaining flour.
4. Divide the dough into 4 equal portions and with the plastic wraps, cover each portion.
5. Refrigerate for at least 2 hours or overnight.
6. For filling in a bowl, add the walnuts, apricots, brown sugar, 1/4 C. plus 2 tbsp of the white sugar and 1/2 tsp of the cinnamon and still till well combined.
7. Set your oven to 425 degrees F and line 2 large baking sheets with 2 greased pieces of the foil.
8. Place 1 portion of the dough onto a lightly floured surface and with a floured rolling pin roll into 9-inch round, keeping remaining dough refrigerated.
9. Spread about 2 tbsp of the raspberry preserves and sprinkle with about 1/2 C. of the apricot filling.
10. Gently press the filling onto dough.
11. With a sharp knife, cut the dough into 12 equal sized wedges.
12. Starting at curved edge, roll up each wedge, jelly-roll fashion.
13. Place cookies onto the prepared cookie sheet, point-side down, about 1/2 inch apart.
14. Repeat with remaining dough, one-fourth at a time.
15. A bowl, mix together the remaining 2 tbsp of the sugar and 1 tsp of the cinnamon.
16. Coat the rugelach with the milk and sprinkle with the cinnamon-sugar.
17. Cook in the oven for about 30-35 minutes.
18. Remove from the oven and immediately, transfer the rugelach onto the wire racks to cool.
19. Store in tightly covered container.

Sweet Cream
Cheese Bread

Prep Time: 15 mins
Total Time: 1 hr 25 mins

Servings per Recipe: 12
Calories	271 kcal
Fat	7.2 g
Carbohydrates	49.1g
Protein	4.6 g
Cholesterol	42 mg
Sodium	304 mg

Ingredients

1 C. boiling water
1 C. dried apricots, chopped
3 tbsp margarine
1/2 C. cream cheese, softened
1 C. white sugar
2 eggs
2 C. all-purpose flour

2 tsp baking powder
1/2 tsp baking soda
1/2 tsp salt
1 C. dates, pitted and chopped

Directions

1. Set your oven to 350 degrees F before doing anything else and grease a 9x5x3-inch loaf pan.
2. In a small bowl, soak the apricots in boiling water and keep aside to cool.
3. In a second bowl, mix together the flour, baking powder, soda, salt and dates.
4. In a large bowl, add the margarine, cream cheese and sugar and beat till creamy.
5. Add the eggs, one at a time and beat till smooth.
6. Stir in the cooled apricots and water.
7. Add the flour mixture and stir till just moistened.
8. Transfer the mixture into the prepared loaf pan.
9. Cook in the oven for about 1 hour or till a toothpick inserted in the center comes out clean.
10. Remove from the oven and cool for about 10 minutes before turning out onto wire rack to cool completely.

YAMS
in December

Prep Time: 20 mins
Total Time: 1 hr 5 mins

Servings per Recipe: 8
Calories	348 kcal
Fat	7.9 g
Carbohydrates	68.4g
Protein	3.5 g
Cholesterol	8 mg
Sodium	196 mg

Ingredients

3 lb. sweet potatoes, peeled and cut into chunks
1 C. packed brown sugar
5 tsp cornstarch
1/4 tsp salt
1/8 tsp ground cinnamon
1 C. apricot nectar
1/2 C. hot water
2 tsp grated orange peel
2 tbsp butter
1/2 C. chopped pecans

Directions

1. In a large pan of water, add the sweet potatoes on high heat and bring to a boil.
2. Reduce the heat to medium-low and simmer, covered for about 20 minutes.
3. Drain and keep aside for about 1-2 minute.
4. Set your oven to 350 degrees F and grease a 13x9-inch baking dish.
5. In a pan, mix together the brown sugar, cornstarch, salt, cinnamon, apricot nectar, water and orange peel on medium heat and bring to a boil.
6. Reduce the heat to medium-low and cook, stirring continuously for about 2 minutes.
7. Stir in the butter and pecans.
8. Arrange the sweet potato chunks into the prepared baking dish and top with the sauce evenly.
9. Cook in the oven for about 25-30 minutes.

Parsi Style
Chicken Curry

Prep Time: 30 mins
Total Time: 1 hr 10 mins

Servings per Recipe: 4

Calories	649 kcal
Fat	23.1 g
Carbohydrates	75.3g
Protein	40.1 g
Cholesterol	117 mg
Sodium	168 mg

Ingredients

8 chicken drumsticks
salt and pepper to taste
2 tbsp olive oil
3 cloves garlic, minced
1/2 tsp red pepper flakes
4 C. apricot nectar
1 tsp cornstarch
1 tbsp water
3 tbsp Madras curry powder
1 C. dried apricots
1 large onion, roughly chopped
1 large green bell pepper, roughly chopped
4 carrots, thinly sliced
1 fresh green chili pepper, minced (optional)
1/2 C. chopped water chestnuts (optional)

Directions

1. Set your oven to 350 degrees F before doing anything else.
2. Season the chicken drumsticks with the salt and pepper.
3. In a large oven-safe skillet, heat the olive oil on medium heat and sauté the garlic and red pepper flakes for about 1-2 minutes.
4. Add the drumsticks and sear for about 3 minutes per side.
5. Transfer the skillet into the oven.
6. Cook in the oven for about 7-10 minutes.
7. In a large pan, add the apricot nectar and bring to a boil on medium-high heat.
8. Meanwhile, in a small bowl, dissolve the cornstarch in water.
9. Reduce the heat to medium-low and stir in the cornstarch mixture and curry powder.
10. Add the dried apricots and stir to combine.
11. Transfer the baked drumsticks into the apricot mixture and remove from the heat.
12. Heat the same skillet used to cook the chicken on medium heat and sauté the onion, green bell pepper, carrots and green chili pepper and cook till the onion becomes softened.
13. Add the drumsticks and apricot sauce and simmer, covered for about 10 minutes.
14. Season with the salt and pepper.
15. Stir in the water chestnuts and serve immediately.

MINCED
Fruit Medley

Prep Time: 10 mins
Total Time: 45 mins

Servings per Recipe: 96
Calories	102 kcal
Fat	0.1 g
Carbohydrates	< 26.6g
Protein	0.5 g
Cholesterol	0 mg
Sodium	26 mg

Ingredients

6 C. white sugar
1 tsp ground cinnamon
1 tsp ground allspice
1 tsp ground cloves
1 tsp salt
8 lb. pears - peeled, cored and chopped
1 large orange, quartered with peel

1 lemon, quartered and seeded
1 tart apple - peeled, cored and chopped
1 C. dried apricots, chopped
1 C. grape juice
1 C. cider vinegar
3 C. raisins
2 1/2 C. dried currants

Directions

1. In a large pan, mix together the sugar, cinnamon, allspice, cloves and salt.
2. Add the pears, orange, lemon, apple and apricot and with a potato masher, mash completely.
3. Stir in the grape juice, vinegar, raisins and currants and bring to a boil on medium heat, stirring occasionally.
4. Simmer till the mixture becomes thick.
5. Place the mixture into hot sterilized jars to within 1/4 inch of jar top and seal.
6. It can be preserved in refrigerator for at least one year.

Brittany
Crusty Cake

🥣 Prep Time: 20 mins
🕐 Total Time: 1 hr

Servings per Recipe: 8
Calories	290 kcal
Fat	10.8 g
Carbohydrates	42.6g
Protein	8.3 g
Cholesterol	23 mg
Sodium	132 mg

Ingredients

10 small fresh apricots, pitted and quartered
1/3 C. white sugar
1 C. almond meal
1/2 C. confectioners' sugar
1 egg
1 (9 inch) refrigerated pie crust (such as

Pillsbury(R))
1/3 C. apricot jam, melted

Directions

1. Set your oven to 350 degrees F before doing anything else.
2. Roll out the pie crust onto a baking sheet.
3. In a bowl, add the quartered apricots and white sugar and toss to coat well.
4. In another bowl, add the almond meal, confectioner's sugar and egg and mix till a paste forms.
5. Spread the almond paste in the center of the pie crust, leaving 1/2-inch of bare crust all around the edge.
6. Arrange the sugared apricots over the almond paste.
7. Fold the 1/2-inch bare edge of the crust inward over the almond paste and apricots, leaving the center of the tart uncovered.
8. Crimp the edge down with a fork as you go around the tart.
9. Cook in the oven for about 40 minutes.
10. Spread the melted apricot jam over the hot galette.
11. Cut into desired slices and serve.

A SIMPLE
Pie of Berry

Prep Time: 15 mins
Total Time: 1 h 5 mins

Servings per Recipe: 8
Calories	366 kcal
Fat	16.6 g
Carbohydrates	52.6g
Protein	3.3 g
Cholesterol	4 mg
Sodium	318 mg

Ingredients
3/4 C. white sugar
3 tbsp cornstarch
1/4 tsp salt
1/2 tsp ground cinnamon
4 C. fresh blueberries
1 recipe pastry for a 9 inch double crust pie
1 tbsp butter

Directions
1. Set your oven to 425 degrees F before doing anything else and arrange the rack in the lower shelfn of oven.
2. In a bowl, place the blueberries, sugar, cornstarch, salt, and cinnamon and gently toss to coat.
3. Line a pie dish with 1 pie crust.
4. Place the blueberry mixture into the crust and top with the butter in the form of dots.
5. Cut remaining pastry into 1/2-3/4-inch wide strips and make a lattice top crust.
6. Crimp and flute the edges.
7. Cook in the oven for about 50 minutes.

American
Blueberry Buckle

🥣 Prep Time: 10 mins
🕐 Total Time: 10 h 10 mins

Servings per Recipe: 10
Calories	319 kcal
Fat	10.8 g
Carbohydrates	52.4g
Protein	4.3 g
Cholesterol	32 mg
Sodium	259 mg

Ingredients

3/4 C. white sugar
1/4 C. shortening
1 egg
1/2 C. milk
2 C. all-purpose flour
2 tsp baking powder
1/2 tsp salt

2 C. fresh blueberries
1/2 C. white sugar
1/3 C. all-purpose flour
1/2 tsp ground cinnamon
1/4 C. butter, softened

Directions

1. Set your oven to 375 degrees F before doing anything else and lightly, grease an 8x8-inch baking dish.
2. In a bowl, add 3/4 C. of the sugar, shortening and egg and beat till creamy.
3. In another bowl mix together 2 C. of the flour, baking powder and salt.
4. Add the flour mixture into the sugar mixture, alternating with milk.
5. Stir in blueberries.
6. Transfer the mixture into the prepared baking dish.
7. For topping in a bowl, mix together 1/2 C. of the sugar, 1/3 C. of the flour, cinnamon and butter.
8. Sprinkle the topping mixture over the cake mixture evenly.
9. Cook in the oven for about 25-30 minutes.

TUESDAY
Lunch Salad

Prep Time: 10 mins
Total Time: 1 h

Servings per Recipe: 15

Calories	248 kcal
Fat	8.5 g
Carbohydrates	41.3g
Protein	2.8 g
Cholesterol	23 mg
Sodium	87 mg

Ingredients

2 (3 oz.) packages raspberry flavored Jell-O(R) mix
2 C. hot water
1 (20 oz.) can crushed pineapple, drained
1 (21 oz.) can blueberry pie filling
1 (8 oz.) package cream cheese
1/2 C. white sugar
1 C. sour cream
1 tsp vanilla extract

Directions

1. In a bowl, add the hot water and gelatin and stir till dissolved.

2. Stir in the pineapple and blueberry pie filling.

3. Transfer the mixture into a 13x9-inch baking dish and refrigerate till firm.

4. In a bowl, add cream cheese and sugar and beat till creamy.

5. Add sour cream and vanilla and beat till well combined.

6. Spread over firm gelatin and refrigerate to chill before serving.

Sunday
Breakfast Bread

Prep Time: 10 mins
Total Time: 50 mins

Servings per Recipe: 12
Calories	266 kcal
Fat	10 g
Carbohydrates	41.4g
Protein	3.5 g
Cholesterol	16 mg
Sodium	231 mg

Ingredients

1/2 C. vegetable oil
1 C. white sugar
3 tbsp molasses
1 egg
2 C. all-purpose flour
1 tsp ground cinnamon
1/2 tsp ground nutmeg

1/2 tsp ground ginger
1 tsp baking soda
1/2 tsp salt
1 C. fresh blueberries
1 C. buttermilk
2 tbsp sugar

Directions

1. Set your oven to 350 degrees F before doing anything else and grease an 11x7-inch baking dish.
2. In a large bowl, add the oil, 1 C. of the sugar and molasses and mix till well combined.
3. Add the egg and beat well.
4. In another bowl, mix together the flour, cinnamon, nutmeg, ginger, baking soda and salt.
5. In a bowl, add 2 tbsp of the flour mixture and blueberries and toss to coat.
6. Add the remaining flour mixture into the oil mixture alternately with the buttermilk, mixing after each addition.
7. Gently, fold in the blueberries.
8. Transfer the mixture into the prepared pan and top with the remaining white sugar.
9. Cook in the oven for about 35-40 minutes or till a toothpick inserted in the center comes out clean.

FRUITY
Cornbread

Prep Time: 15 mins
Total Time: 40 mins

Servings per Recipe: 6
Calories	453 kcal
Fat	21.3 g
Carbohydrates	59.8g
Protein	7.2 g
Cholesterol	64 mg
Sodium	668 mg

Ingredients
1 C. cornmeal
1 C. all-purpose flour
1/2 C. white sugar
3 tsp baking powder
1 tsp salt
2 eggs
2/3 C. milk
1/2 C. vegetable oil

2 C. blueberries

Directions
1. Set your oven to 400 degrees F before doing anything else and grease a 9-inch square baking dish.
2. In a bowl, mix together the cornmeal, flour, sugar, baking powder and salt.
3. In another bowl, add the eggs, milk and oil and beat well.
4. Add the cornmeal mixture into the egg mixture and mix till just combined.
5. Fold in the blueberries.
6. Transfer the mixture into the prepared baking dish.
7. Cook in the oven for about 25-30 minutes or till a toothpick inserted in the center comes out clean.w

76   Fruity Cornbread

Versatile
Vanilla Blueberry Bread

Prep Time: 10 mins
Total Time: 1 h 10 mins

Servings per Recipe: 12
Calories	168 kcal
Fat	5.4 g
Carbohydrates	27.8g
Protein	2.6 g
Cholesterol	16 mg
Sodium	116 mg

Ingredients
1 1/2 C. all-purpose flour
3/4 C. white sugar
2 tsp baking powder
1/8 tsp salt
1/2 C. milk
1/4 C. vegetable oil
1 egg

1/2 tsp vanilla extract
1 1/2 C. blueberries

Directions
1. Set your oven to 350 degrees F before doing anything else and grease a loaf pan.
2. In a large bowl, mix together the flour, sugar, baking powder and salt.
3. Add the milk, oil, egg and vanilla extract and mix till just combined.
4. Gently fold in the blueberries.
5. Transfer the mixture into the prepared loaf pan.
6. Cook in the oven for about 60-70 minutes or till a toothpick inserted in the center comes out clean.

CRESCENT ROLL
Blueberry Turnovers

Prep Time: 10 mins
Total Time: 27 mins

Servings per Recipe: 8

Calories	159 kcal
Fat	7.2 g
Carbohydrates	20.8g
Protein	2.1 g
Cholesterol	0 mg
Sodium	233 mg

Ingredients

1 (8 oz.) package refrigerated crescent rolls
1/2 C. fresh blueberries
1/4 C. confectioners' sugar
1/4 C. prepared vanilla frosting (optional)

Directions

1. Set your oven to 375 degrees F before doing anything else.
2. Roll out the crescent dough triangles onto a baking sheet.
3. Place 1 tbsp blueberries on the widest end of each triangle and sprinkle with 1/2 tsp of the confectioners' sugar.
4. Beginning with the wide end, roll up each crescent around blueberries and pinch both sides to seal completely.
5. Cook in the oven for about 12 minutes.
6. Remove from the oven and keep on a wire rack to cool for ab out 5 minutes.
7. Dust with the remaining confectioners' sugar and drizzle with the vanilla frosting before using.

Ethan's Blueberry Cream Cheese Dessert

🥣 Prep Time: 15 mins
🕐 Total Time: 4 h 15 mins

Servings per Recipe: 10
Calories	450 kcal
Fat	19.9 g
Carbohydrates	63.6g
Protein	5.3 g
Cholesterol	27 mg
Sodium	346 mg

Ingredients

1 (10 inch) angel food cake
1 (8 oz.) package cream cheese
1 C. milk
1 (16 oz.) package frozen whipped topping, thawed
1 (21 oz.) can blueberry pie filling
1/2 C. confectioners' sugar

1/2 tsp vanilla extract

Directions

1. Break the angel food cake into small pieces
2. In the bottom of a 13x9-inch baking dish, place the cake pieces.
3. In a bowl, add the confectioners' sugar, cream cheese, vanilla and milk and mix till smooth.
4. Fold in the whipped topping and spread over the cake pieces evenly.
5. Top with the blueberries evenly and refrigerate to chill for about 4 hours or overnight.

AUGUST'S BLUEBERRY
Lime-Ade

 Prep Time: 5 mins

Total Time: 5 mins

Servings per Recipe: 8

Calories	72 kcal
Fat	0.1 g
Carbohydrates	< 18.6g
Protein	0.3 g
Cholesterol	< 0 mg
Sodium	6 mg

Ingredients
2 C. fresh blueberries
1/2 C. white sugar
1/3 C. freshly squeezed lime juice
6 C. water

Directions
1. In a blender, add the blueberries, sugar, lime juice and 1 C. of the water and pulse till smooth.
2. Transfer the mixture into a pitcher.
3. Add the remaining water and stir to combine.

Delicious
Morning Smoothie

Prep Time: 5 mins
Total Time: 5 mins

Servings per Recipe: 2
Calories	205 kcal
Fat	1.5 g
Carbohydrates	42.3g
Protein	6.4 g
Cholesterol	6 mg
Sodium	103 mg

Ingredients
1 1/4 C. Ocean Spray(R) Blueberry Juice
Cocktail, chilled
3/4 C. Ocean Spray(R) Fresh Blueberries,
cleaned and rinsed
1 C. vanilla yogurt

Directions
1. In a blender, add the blueberry juice cocktail and blueberries and pulse till smooth.
2. Add the yogurt and pulse till well combined.

EMILY'S
Simple Torte

Prep Time: 15 mins
Total Time: 5 h 15 mins

Servings per Recipe: 12

Calories	408 kcal
Fat	17.9 g
Carbohydrates	59.5g
Protein	3.3 g
Cholesterol	41 mg
Sodium	256 mg

Ingredients

2 (4.8 oz.) packages graham crackers, crushed
1/2 C. butter, melted
1/2 C. white sugar
1 (8 oz.) package cream cheese, softened
1 C. confectioners' sugar
1 C. whipped topping (such as Cool Whip(R))

1 (21 oz.) can blueberry pie filling

Directions

1. In a bowl, mix together the graham crackers, butter and white sugar.
2. Place the mixture in the bottom of a 13x9‑‑inch baking dish and gently, press to smooth.
3. Refrigerate the crust for about 1 hour.
4. In a bowl, add the cream cheese and confectioners' sugar and beat till light and fluffy.
5. Fold in the whipped topping.
6. Spread the cream cheese mixture over the crust evenly and top with the blueberry pie filling.
7. Refrigerate to chill for about 4 hours or overnight.

Blueberry Spritzer

🥣 Prep Time: 15 mins
🕐 Total Time: 4 h 15 mins

Servings per Recipe: 4
Calories	149 kcal
Fat	0.3 g
Carbohydrates	< 38.5g
Protein	0.7 g
Cholesterol	0 mg
Sodium	2 mg

Ingredients
2 1/2 C. blueberries
1/2 C. white sugar
3/4 C. water
1 tbsp fresh lemon juice

Directions
1. In a food processor, add the blueberries and sugar and pulse till smooth.
2. Through a fine-mesh strainer, strain the mixture by pressing with a wooden spoon.
3. In a shallow glass baking dish, add the strained blueberry puree, water and lemon juice and stir to combine.
4. Freeze for about 4 hours, scraping and stirring with a fork after every 1 hour.
5. Just before serving, scrape to fluff and lighten the ice crystals.
6. Transfer into the chilled glasses to serve.

BLUEBERRY WAFER
Dessert Casserole

Prep Time: 15 mins
Total Time: 2 h 15 mins

Servings per Recipe: 8
Calories	449 kcal
Fat	24.3 g
Carbohydrates	54.8g
Protein	3.8 g
Cholesterol	72 mg
Sodium	158 mg

Ingredients
24 vanilla wafers, crushed
1 (8 oz.) package cream cheese, softened
1 C. heavy cream
1/2 C. confectioners' sugar
1 (21 oz.) can blueberry pie filling

Directions
1. In the bottom of a square baking dish, spread the crushed vanilla wafers evenly.
2. In a bowl, add the cream cheese, heavy cream and confectioners' sugar and beat till smooth.
3. Spread the cream cheese mixture over the vanilla wafers evenly.
4. Spread the blueberry pie filling over the cream cheese mixture evenly.
5. Freeze for at least 2 hours before serving.

Pineapple
Berry Crunch

Prep Time: 15 mins
Total Time: 50 mins

Servings per Recipe: 6
Calories	345 kcal
Fat	8.8 g
Carbohydrates	64.7g
Protein	4.3 g
Cholesterol	20 mg
Sodium	284 mg

Ingredients

2 C. fresh blueberries
1 1/2 C. pineapple chunks with juice
1 1/2 tsp all-purpose flour
Topping:
1 C. all-purpose flour
3/4 C. quick-cooking oats
2/3 C. dark brown sugar

3/4 tsp ground cinnamon
3/4 tsp sea salt
1/4 C. melted butter

Directions

1. Set your oven to 350 degrees F before doing anything else.
2. In a pan, mix together the blueberries, pineapple chunks with juice and 1 1/2 tsp of the flour on medium heat and cook for about 5 minutes, stirring continuously.
3. Place the blueberry mixture into an 8-inch baking dish evenly.
4. In a bowl, mix together 1 C. of the flour, oats, brown sugar, cinnamon and sea salt.
5. Add the butter and mix till the topping is crumbly.
6. Spread the topping over blueberry mixture evenly.
7. Cook in the oven or about 30-35 minutes.

A SIMPLE
Flummery

Prep Time: 20 mins
Total Time: 40 mins

Servings per Recipe: 6

Calories	490 kcal
Fat	12.4 g
Carbohydrates	88g
Protein	9.1 g
Cholesterol	10 mg
Sodium	725 mg

Ingredients

1 (3.5 oz.) package instant vanilla pudding mix
2 C. cold milk
2 pints fresh blueberries
1/2 C. white sugar
2 C. all-purpose flour
1 tbsp baking powder
1 tbsp white sugar
1/2 tsp salt

1/4 C. vegetable oil
1 C. milk

Directions

1. In a bowl, add the pudding and 2 C. of the milk and beat till thickened.
2. Refrigerate the pudding before serving.
3. In a large pan, mix together the blueberries and 1/2 C. of the sugar on medium heat.
4. Add enough water that just barely covers the blueberries and bring to a boil.
5. Reduce the heat to low and simmer while you make the biscuits.
6. For the drop biscuits in a bowl, mix together the flour, baking powder, 1 tbsp of the sugar and salt.
7. Make a well in the center of the flour mixture.
8. In the well, add the vegetable oil and 1 C. of the milk and mix till a soft dough forms.
9. Bring the berry mixture back to a boil on medium-low heat.
10. With heaping spoonfuls, place the biscuit dough into the boiling blueberry mixture and simmer, covered for about 15 minutes.
11. Divide the biscuits into serving bowls and top with the blueberry sauce.
12. Serve with a topping of the chilled vanilla pudding.

Thursday's Before Work Oatmeal

Prep Time: 10 mins
Total Time: 15 mins

Servings per Recipe: 2

Calories	210 kcal
Fat	5.6 g
Carbohydrates	33.3g
Protein	6.9 g
Cholesterol	5 mg
Sodium	229 mg

Ingredients

1 1/3 C. water
1 pinch salt
2/3 C. quick oats
1 tbsp crushed flax seed
1 tbsp brown sugar
1 tsp ground cinnamon
1 tsp vanilla extract

1/2 C. milk (optional)
1/4 C. fresh blueberries

Directions

1. In a pan, add the water and salt and bring to a boil.
2. Add the oats and cook for about 2-3 minutes.
3. Stir in the flax, brown sugar, cinnamon and vanilla extract and cook for about 2-3 minutes more.
4. Stir in the milk and blueberries and serve.

LEMON PEEL
Topping

Prep Time: 5 mins
Total Time: 20 mins

Servings per Recipe: 8
Calories	390 kcal
Fat	0.6 g
Carbohydrates	< 100.5g
Protein	1.3 g
Cholesterol	0 mg
Sodium	2 mg

Ingredients
2 quarts blueberries, rinsed and drained
2 C. water
1 tbsp grated lemon peel
3 C. white sugar
4 C. water
2 tbsp lemon juice

Directions
1. In a large pan, add the blueberries on low heat and with a potato masher, crush them.
2. Add the water and lemon peel and simmer for about 5 minutes.
3. Through a cheese cloth, strain fruit and reserve the juice.
4. In a large pan, mix together the sugar and 4 C. water and bring to a boil, stirring occasionally till the temperature reaches to 260 degrees F.
5. Add the blueberry juice and boil for about 1 minute.
6. Stir in the lemon juice and remove from the heat.
7. Keep aside to cool.

Blueberry Bread
Custard Bake

Prep Time: 20 mins
Total Time: 9 h 20 mins

Servings per Recipe: 16

Calories	369 kcal
Fat	15.8 g
Carbohydrates	46.9g
Protein	11.4 g
Cholesterol	176 mg
Sodium	342 mg

Ingredients

Strata:
cooking spray
1 loaf French bread, cubed
1 1/2 C. blueberries
2 (8 oz.) packages cream cheese, cut into
1/2-inch cubes
12 eggs
1/3 C. maple syrup

2 C. milk
Blueberry Syrup:
1 1/2 C. white sugar
3 tbsp cornstarch
1 1/2 C. water
1 1/2 C. fresh blueberries
1 1/2 tbsp butter

Directions

1. Grease a 13x9-inch baking dish with the cooking spray.
2. Place 1/2 of the bread cubes into the prepared baking dish and top with 1 1/2 C. of the blueberries.
3. Spread the cream cheese over the blueberries evenly and top with the remaining bread cubes.
4. In a bowl, add the eggs, maple syrup and milk and beat till well combined.
5. Place the egg mixture over the bread cubes evenly.
6. Refrigerate, covered for overnight.
7. Set your oven to 350 degrees F.
8. Cover the baking dish and cook in the oven for about 30 minutes.
9. Uncover and cook in the oven for about 30 minutes more.
10. Meanwhile for the blueberry syrup in a pan, mix together the sugar, cornstarch and water on high heat and bring to a boil over high heat.
11. Cook for 5 minutes. Add the remaining 1 1/2 C. of the blueberries and cook for about 10 minutes.
12. Remove from the heat and stir in the butter. Serve warm over the strata slices.

BERRY
Squares

Prep Time: 20 mins
Total Time: 2 h 15 mins

Servings per Recipe: 24
Calories	146 kcal
Fat	5.2 g
Carbohydrates	22.7g
Protein	2.4 g
Cholesterol	0 mg
Sodium	136 mg

Ingredients

1 (14 oz.) can chickpeas (garbanzo beans), drained and rinsed
1/2 C. rolled oats
1/2 C. brown sugar
1/4 C. olive oil
2 tsp vanilla extract
1 tsp baking powder
1/4 tsp baking soda
1/4 tsp salt
3 C. blueberries
2 tbsp white sugar

1 tbsp lemon juice
2 tbsp cornstarch
1/4 C. cold water
1 1/2 C. rolled oats
1 C. all-purpose flour
1/2 C. brown sugar
1/4 C. olive oil
1 tsp vanilla extract
1/2 tsp baking soda

Directions

1. Set your oven to 350 degrees F before doing anything else.
2. In a food processor, add the chickpeas, 1/2 C. of the rolled oats, 1/2 C. of the brown sugar, 1/4 C. of the olive oil, 2 tsp of the vanilla extract, baking powder, 1/4 tsp of the baking soda and salt and pulse till a dough-like mixture forms.
3. Place the dough into an 8x11-inch baking dish and press to smooth.
4. Cook in the oven for about 20 minutes.
5. In a pan, mix together the blueberries, white sugar and lemon juice on medium-low heat and cook for about 10-15 minutes.
6. In a small bowl, dissolve the cornstarch in water.
7. Add the cornstarch mixture into the pan, stirring continuously and cook for about 2-3 minutes.
8. Place the blueberry mixture over the cooked crust evenly.
9. In a large bowl, add 1 1/2 C. of the rolled oats, flour, 1/2 C. of the brown sugar, 1/4 C. of the olive oil, 1 tsp of the vanilla extract and 1/2 tsp of the baking soda together and mix till the bread crumb like texture forms.
10. Spread the oats mixture over the blueberry mixture evenly.
11. Cook in the oven for about 20 minutes. Remove from the oven and keep aside to cool.
12. Cut into equal sized squares.

Big Ben
Blueberry Cookies

Prep Time: 10 mins
Total Time: 1 h 50 mins

Servings per Recipe: 12	
Calories	252 kcal
Fat	9 g
Carbohydrates	39 g
Protein	4.2 g
Cholesterol	52 mg
Sodium	152 mg

Ingredients

2 1/2 C. all-purpose flour
2 tsp baking powder
1 pinch salt
1/2 C. butter
1 C. white sugar
2 eggs, beaten
1/2 tsp lemon extract
1/2 C. milk
1 C. fresh blueberries

Directions

1. Set your oven to 375 degrees F before doing anything else and grease cookie sheets.
2. In a bowl, sift together the flour, baking powder and salt.
3. In another large bowl, add the butter and sugar and beat till creamy.
4. Add the eggs and lemon flavoring and beat till well combined.
5. Add the milk and flour mixture alternately in three parts, starting with the milk.
6. Gently, fold in the blueberries.
7. With tbsp, place the mixture onto the prepared cookie sheets about 1 1/2-inch apart.
8. Cook in the oven for about 12-15 minutes.

BERRY FRUITY
Salsa

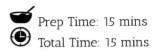

Prep Time: 15 mins
Total Time: 15 mins

Servings per Recipe: 24

Calories	13 kcal
Fat	< 0.1 g
Carbohydrates	< 3.2g
Protein	0.2 g
Cholesterol	< 0 mg
Sodium	23 mg

Ingredients
2 C. chopped fresh blueberries
1 C. whole fresh blueberries
1 tbsp finely chopped jalapeno pepper
1/3 C. chopped red onion
1/4 C. chopped red bell pepper
1 fresh lime, juiced
salt to taste

Directions
1. In a bowl, mix together the chopped and whole blueberries, jalapeño pepper, onion, red pepper, lime juice and salt.

Crackers & Blueberries

Prep Time: 25 mins
Total Time: 1 h

Servings per Recipe: 12
Calories	363 kcal
Fat	19 g
Carbohydrates	45.9 g
Protein	3.3 g
Cholesterol	48 mg
Sodium	156 mg

Ingredients

1/2 C. softened butter
26 saltine crackers, crushed
1/2 C. chopped walnuts
4 large egg whites
1 C. white sugar
1 tsp cream of tartar
1 tsp white vinegar

1 tsp vanilla extract
1 (21 oz.) can blueberry pie filling
1 tsp lemon juice
1 C. heavy cream
1/2 tsp vanilla extract
2 tbsp confectioners' sugar

Directions

1. Set your oven to 350 degrees F before doing anything else.
2. In a bowl, add the butter, crushed saltines and walnuts and mix till well combined.
3. In the bottom of an 12x8-inch baking dish, place the butter mixture and press to smooth.
4. In a large glass bowl, add the egg whites, sugar, cream of tartar and vinegar and with an electric mixer, beat till the stiff peaks form.
5. Add 1 tsp of the vanilla extract and beat till combined.
6. Spread the meringue mixture over the prepared crust evenly.
7. Cook in the oven for about 10-15 minutes.
8. Remove from the oven and keep aside to cool.
9. In a bowl, mix together the blueberry pie filling and lemon juice.
10. Place the pie filling mixture over the cooled meringue evenly.
11. In a bowl, add the cream and 1/2 tsp of the vanilla extract and with an electric mixer, beat, slowly adding the confectioners' sugar till the fluffy peaks form.
12. Spread the whipped cream mixture over the pie filling mixture evenly.
13. Refrigerate before serving.

THURSDAY'S BLUEBERRY
Orange Chicken

Prep Time: 10 mins
Total Time: 35 mins

Servings per Recipe: 4

Calories	233 kcal
Fat	6.7 g
Carbohydrates	17.6g
Protein	24.9 g
Cholesterol	67 mg
Sodium	252 mg

Ingredients
2 tbsp Dijon mustard
2 tbsp orange marmalade
1 tbsp olive oil
4 skinless, boneless chicken breast halves
2 C. frozen blueberries, thawed

salt and ground black pepper to taste
1/2 C. white vinegar

Directions
1. In a bowl, mix together the mustard and marmalade.
2. In a skillet, heat the olive oil on medium heat and cook the chicken for about 5 minutes per side.
3. Place the mustard mixture over the chicken evenly and add the blueberries to the skillet.
4. Cook for about 10 minutes, stirring occasionally.
5. Transfer the chicken into a serving plate.
6. In the same skillet, add the vinegar into blueberry mixture with salt and pepper and cook for about 5-10 minutes, stirring occasionally.
7. Serve the chicken with a topping of the blueberry sauce.   In a bowl, mix together the mustard and marmalade.
8. In a skillet, heat the olive oil on medium heat and cook the chicken for about 5 minutes per side.
9. Place the mustard mixture over the chicken evenly and add the blueberries to the skillet.
10. Cook for about 10 minutes, stirring occasionally.
11. Transfer the chicken into a serving plate.
12. In the same skillet, add the vinegar into blueberry mixture with salt and pepper and cook for about 5-10 minutes, stirring occasionally.
13. Serve the chicken with a topping of the blueberry sauce.

Whipped Pecan
Buttery Berry Dessert

Prep Time: 10 mins
Total Time: 1 h 20 mins

Servings per Recipe: 8

Calories	900 kcal
Fat	47.5 g
Carbohydrates	109.8g
Protein	9.4 g
Cholesterol	110 mg
Sodium	311 mg

Ingredients
1 1/2 C. all-purpose flour
3/4 C. butter
1 C. chopped pecans
2 (8 oz.) packages cream cheese
3 C. confectioners' sugar
1/2 tsp vanilla extract
2 (1.3 oz.) envelopes whipped topping mix

1 C. milk
1 (21 oz.) can blueberry pie filling

Directions
1. Set your oven to 325 degrees F before doing anything else.
2. Place the mixture into a 13x9-inch baking dish.
3. Cook in the oven for about 30 minutes.
4. Remove from the oven and keep aside to cool.
5. In a large bowl, add the cream cheese, confectioners' sugar, vanilla, whipped topping mix and milk and with an electric mixer, beat at high speed till smooth.
6. Place the mixture over the baked crust.
7. Refrigerate to chill before serving.
8. Serve with a topping of the blueberry pie filling.

HOMEMADE
Blueberry Jam

Prep Time: 10 mins
Total Time: 12 h 15 mins

Servings per Recipe: 16
Calories   20 kcal
Fat   0.1 g
Carbohydrates   < 5g
Protein   0.3 g
Cholesterol   < 0 mg
Sodium   < 1 mg

Ingredients
2 C. fresh blueberries
3/4 C. water, divided
2 tsp lemon juice
1 1/2 tsp unflavored gelatin
3 tbsp white sugar

Directions
1. In a heavy pan, mix together the blueberries, 1/2 C. of the water and lemon juice on medium-high heat and bring to a boil.
2. Reduce the heat and simmer for about 8 minutes, stirring occasionally.
3. Meanwhile, dissolve the gelatin in 1/4 C. of the cold water.
4. Remove the blueberries from the heat and stir in the gelatin and sugar.
5. Transfer the mixture into hot, sterilized jars and seal.
6. Cool and store in the refrigerator.

Blueberry
Brunch

🥣 Prep Time: 10 mins

🕐 Total Time: 40 mins

Servings per Recipe: 6
Calories	258 kcal
Fat	9.8 g
Carbohydrates	36.1g
Protein	6.8 g
Cholesterol	112 mg
Sodium	93 mg

Ingredients

3 tbsp butter, cut into 6 equal-sized pieces
1 C. whole milk
3 eggs, beaten
1/4 C. white sugar
1 tsp vanilla extract

1 C. all-purpose flour
1/2 C. fresh blueberries
1 tbsp white sugar
1 tsp ground cinnamon
1/4 C. confectioners' sugar
1 lemon, halved

Directions

1. Set your oven to 375 degrees F before doing anything else and place a piece of butter in 6 cups of a large muffin pan.
2. Place the muffin pan in the preheated oven for about 5 minutes.
3. In a large bowl, add the milk, eggs, 1/4 C. of the sugar and vanilla and beat till well combined.
4. Add the flour into the milk mixture and mix till well combined.
5. Transfer the mixture into the muffin cups evenly.
6. Place the blueberries into each muffin mixture evenly.
7. In a small bowl, mix together 1 tbsp of the sugar and cinnamon.
8. Sprinkle the sugar mixture over each muffin mixture evenly.
9. Cook in the oven for about 5 minutes.
10. Now, set the oven to 350 degrees F.
11. Cook in the oven for about 25 minutes or till a toothpick inserted in the center comes out clean.
12. Dust confectioners' sugar on top of each popover.
13. Serve warm with a drizzling of the lemon juice.

Apricot Leather

 Prep Time: 30 mins

Total Time: 6 hr 30 mins

Servings per Recipe: 14

Calories	39 kcal
Fat	0.1 g
Carbohydrates	< 9.8g
Protein	0.3 g
Cholesterol	< 0 mg
Sodium	< 1 mg

Ingredients

1 tsp lemon juice
2 C. pitted and diced fresh apricots
1/2 C. white sugar

Directions

1. Set your oven to 150 degrees F before doing anything else and line a 17x11-inch cookie sheet with a piece of plastic wrap.
2. In a pan, mix together the lemon juice, apricots and sugar on medium heat and cook till the sugar is dissolved.
3. Remove from the heat and cool lightly.
4. Transfer the apricot mixture into a blender and pulse till smooth.
5. Spread the pureed fruit mixture onto the prepared cookie sheet evenly within 1-inch of the edge.
6. Cook in the oven for about 4-6 hours, using a spoon to keep the door slightly ajar.
7. After drying, cut it into strips and store in an airtight container.